Deer Ma

Manage Your Way To Better Deer Hunting

by

Dr. Grant Woods
Bryan Kinkel
Robert Bennett

Woods and Associates, Inc.

Foreword
by
Walt Hampton

Preface
by
Patrick Durkin

Woods and Associates Publications

Published by
Woods and Associates, Inc.
4792 East State Highway 248
Reeds Spring, Missouri 65737

Front Cover Design and Photograph
George Barnett

Back Cover Photographs
George Barnett
Kent Hensley

ISBN: 0-9746968-0-3

Library of Congress Control Number: 2004090893

Praise for

Deer Management 101

Manage Your Way to Better Hunting

"Deer Management 101 is a superb book, written by men who know their craft as well as anyone in the business. If you have a desire to further your knowledge on whitetail management, this is the book to have. It should be required reading for all deer hunters, it's that good."

-Charles J. Alsheimer
Northern Field Editor
Deer & Deer Hunting magazine

"...Great effort on the part of the authors in producing what is an easy reading book covering some quite technical aspects to deer management. It always staggers me that as I learn more and more about whitetail herd management in North America, from particularly Dr. Grant Woods, I recognize the many similarities with domesticated deer farming in New Zealand. So many of the principles discussed and explained about whitetail herd management, hold true for our deer farming management in New Zealand. The area with which I am most familiar is quality forages and nutrition. Here in New Zealand farming we have the adage about animal productivity "10% breeding, 90% feeding." Likewise for white-tailed deer, I expect that where all else is managed, deer nutrition and the provision of forages that match nutritional demands of deer during the year is key, as alluded to several times throughout the book..."

-Bruce Garrett
Research Biologist
Wrightson Seed, New Zealand

"Deer Management 101 should be on the bookshelf of every serious whitetail hunter. Grant Woods is not only one of our country's top authorities on whitetail biology and management, he's also an astute and successful hunter. That rare combination makes him the perfect candidate to write this book. DM101 provides solid, logical, science-based strategies for the hunter/landowner wanting to maximize the potential of whitetails and their habitat."

-Scott Bestul
Contributing Editor
Field & Stream magazine

"Grant Woods should have been a teacher--this book is straightforward, no-nonsense biology in a conversational form easily digested by professionals or those new to the world of whitetail deer. This is sure to be the deer management textbook of the new Century."

-Walt Hampton
Southern Field Editor
Deer and Deer Hunting magazine

"A more knowledgeable deer-herd manager you'll never find. Dr. Grant Woods has taken the complex science of quality herd management and made it make sense, allowing every hunter and landowner to get the most out of their land and deer population."

-A.E. Walsh
Publisher
American Hunter magazine

"Dr. Grant Woods understands that today's deer hunters crave in-depth, hands-on information about white-tailed deer. Not only has Dr. Woods pioneered new research techniques to obtain hard-core insights into whitetail behavior, but he also knows how to make his findings understandable and relevant to deer hunters everywhere. This book showcases his talents as a keen observer of deer and their habitats and reveals how hunters can put those insights to work on their hunting lands."

-Patrick Durkin
Editor
National Whitetail Hunter's Journal
former Editor
Deer & Deer Hunting magazine:

"Grant Woods and his co-authors have spent their professional lives working with deer and translating deer research into practice. They know what works in the field and what doesn't. Their book is the perfect mix of research and practice. It should be a part of every deer enthusiast's library and referred to regularly. I wish we had this book before we started our management program."

-Craig Dougherty
Co-founder
NorthCountry Whitetails

"Grant Woods brings his readers to a new level of hunting maturity. Within every sentence, this book is brimming with information and education on the wise use and future stewardship of our deer resource. Woods poignantly helps hunters realize that their management role is much bigger than their/our own self righteousness. Whereby shooting adult does is more of an obligation to the land than to their own self-interests. This book is the next Bible on Deer Management 101."

-C.J. Winand
"Huntin' Whitetails" Columnist
Bowhunter magazine

Dedication

This book is dedicated to our families.

Thank you for your love, and for allowing us to vigorously pursue our obsession with whitetails.

Table of Contents

Table of Contents

Foreword

There are several books on "homemade" deer management on the shelves, and up until now, what they all have in common is the oversimplification of a technical scientific topic that still today baffles wildlife biology professionals. Managing a deer herd or managing a tract of land for deer is not an "out of the box," one-size-fits-all proposition. Finally, a true deer management professional and respected biologist has put his considerable knowledge on the subject in a format and language that anyone interested in whitetail deer can understand. This book, *Deer Management 101 - Manage Your Way To Better Hunting* has hit the mark the others have missed.

To be a successful hunter one must know his game. To be a successful manager one must know the land. At last, a true scientist and wildlife professional has put the two together. The result is a work sure to be the new textbook for deer hunters in the new century.

Dr. Grant Woods is one of the most respected wildlife biologists in America, well-known among his peers for his outstanding real-world-applicable research and unique understanding of the deer-habitat relationship. Grant, a devoted deer hunter and wonderful public speaker, has now taken that enthusiasm and energy and transmitted it into a body of work sure to be the deer management book by which all others will be judged. In his step-by-step approach to the subject, Dr. Woods builds a firm foundation for understanding the complex relationship between deer and the land; by so doing, he reaps for the hunter/manager a wealth of deer know-how that is sure to be responsible for many successful hunts. In concise, understandable language this work deals with the animal, the land, and where the relationship can most benefit the deer hunter.

In my own library are dozens of books dealing with deer. Most are virtually useless in real-world application. My only suggestion to Grant is to print his book in a three-ring binder format--I expect to wear out the binding using his work for my own managing, teaching and hunting! If you are a deer person and want to finally get into the meat of management, want to take your hunting success to the next level, and want to truly understand the deer-land relationship I can recommend no better place to start than with *Deer Management 101 - Manage Your Way To Better Hunting*.

-Walt Hampton
Southern Field Editor
***Deer and Deer Hunting** magazine*

Preface

When considering how deer hunting and whitetail management have changed in the 30-some years I've been toting a bow and gun, it sometimes seems we're talking about different animals and different human expectations.

I didn't realize it at the time, but when I started deer hunting in 1971 the overriding scheme in deer management was the opening sentence in Aldo Leopold's book, Game Management: "Game management is the art of making land produce sustained annual crops of wild game for recreational use."

Wildlife managers for much of the 1900s were viewed as public servants who could provide wildlife-based recreation for the nation's sportsmen. They worked tirelessly, and at low pay, to restore wildlife populations that had been decimated by uncontrolled habitat destruction and unregulated hunting, both subsistence and commercial. As the nation's woodlands and other wild places regrew, wildlife managers helped restore whitetails and myriad other species. Their efforts were so successful that by the final quarter of the 1900s, the land was producing far larger annual supplies of white-tailed deer than traditional recreational hunting regulations could control.

Some hunters realized by the late 1980s that the deer woods had changed, and deer management required more from them than occasional recreation. Stewardship of America's favorite wildlife species, the white-tailed deer, suddenly required mixing responsibility to the resource into our recreational pursuits. Wildlife managers appealed for hunters to increasingly play the role of predators in nature's balancing act with this large-bodied prey species. Some hunters understood, of course, and others didn't. Some viewed this as a demand for citizen-hunters to be the servant of wildlife managers and-in effect-big government, or large land-owning corporations.

Even so, this evolution from wildlife managers being the hunter's servants to a perception of hunters being the managers' servants is nowhere near complete, absolute or universal. Like the whitetail and its myriad habitats, it's an ever-changing, or dynamic, process. Managing this publicly owned resource is complicated enough on public lands, but it's even more difficult on private properties. The whitetail's landscape is complicated further by urban sprawl, disappearing family farms, increasingly subdivided rural properties, and an American culture that values individual independence more than cooperation with government and its agencies.

But rather than lament these challenges, some hunters and wildlife managers realize there's endless potential for responsible recreation-or fun-in white-tailed deer management. They don't look at the ever-changing face of deer management and ask, "Why." They look around, envision what's possible, and ask, "Why not?"

For instance, more hunters than ever before not only buy land for deer hunting, they seek ways to help their land produce deer that can achieve their full genetic potential. In many cases, these are people who never gardened or regularly planted trees, let alone operated chain saws and drove tractors. Suddenly, though, because of deer hunting, they realize land management can be fun and rewarding. For the first time they're understanding why some people get such great satisfaction from growing their own crops, or watching trees they've planted put on new growth each summer. These deer hunters look at their land from a new perspective, and realize that Leopold guy was onto something when he said the ax and fire can inspire life, not just take it away. As this newfound appreciation invigorates hunters, they search for ways to interact with their land and the whitetails that call it home.

Even so, most hunters can use some help in wringing maximum production from their hunting properties. That's where people like Dr. Grant Woods, Bryan Kinkel, Robert Bennett and the rest of the Woods and Associates team members fit in. These wildlife managers cater to deer-hunting landowners who want to be actively involved in land and deer management on their properties. As I write this preface in February 2004, Woods and Associates team has already spent more than 15 years traveling across whitetail country to help their clients set up fun, responsible deer-management programs that fit into each particular state's deer hunting regulations.

The results of those first 15 years of private-lands consulting work come to life in this book, *Deer Management 101: Manage Your Way to Better Hunting*. Inside you'll discover why it's possible to have too many deer on your property, and how plants and trees can tell you when deer are living beyond the land's means. You'll also discover why some habitats produce better deer than others, and whether you can do anything to change it. The more you read, the more you'll also appreciate why Leopold called wildlife management an art, not necessarily a science. But make no mistake: Without basic knowledge of the science behind land and wildlife management, artwork isn't possible. By reading this book, you'll better understand your land and how deer will respond to management efforts. As a result, you'll make better decisions on which long-term management programs to apply.

You'll also benefit from the team's vast knowledge of whitetail research, and how and why it's relevant to deer on your property. So often when hunters are asked to comment or make suggestions on deer-management programs, they don't have the benefit of knowing the full background and research underlying the proposals. This book explains basic relationships between deer and their habitat, and how each piece of this puzzle changes the outcomes of programs hunters often ponder. Never before have these relationships been explained in such a clear, common-sense way. Even if you don't own land to manage, this book helps you better understand the art of deer management, and how this knowledge can make your hunts even more enjoyable in the future.

In effect, this book and the Woods and Associates team are a celebration of the cooperative spirit that will always be required for successful deer management. It helps us step back from the political battles and petrified opinions that often plague the deer woods, and realize we would all have more fun if we listened and learned from each other, instead of debating who's the servant and who's the beneficiary. In truth, deer hunting and deer management is about being both, and the more we work on our lands and with each other, the more great recreation we'll enjoy in whitetail country.

-Patrick Durkin, February 2004
Waupaca, Wisconsin

Acknowledgments

The way of a fool seems right to him, but a wise man listens to advice.

Proverbs 12:15 (NIV)

We aren't wise, but we know enough to surround ourselves with friends who are. We are grateful to all the people whose assistance made this book possible. Special thanks go to Dr. Karl Miller and Patrick Durkin for editorial suggestions that made this book far more pleasant to read. Many others added their editorial skills to this project, including Will Andre, Alice Avery, Michael Hanback, Lisa Kinkel, Dr. Larry Marchinton, Lindsey Thomas, Abe Walsh, and Tracy Woods.

We also want to thank the following contributors for sharing their photographs, expertise, and research. George Barnett provided most of the photographs in this book, and the cover design. He also served as the photographic editor. Ms. Jack Branch, Joe Hamilton, Kent Hensley, Dr. Mick Hellickson, Dr. Harry Jacobson, Dr. Larry Marchinton, George Peacon, Ole Torgersen, and Jim Winch also provided photographs. Thanks to Dr. W.J. Bennett Jr. and John Riggs for their Native American archaeological information; to Goose Gosnell, who conducted the literature review of Native American deer harvest data; and John D. Northrip, who provided archaeological photographs.

Members of Woods and Associates include Grant Adkinson, Kendall Alley, Terry Baxter, Hank Bergstrom, Brian Bish, Gregg Brown, Brett Collins, Steve Dover, Rob Freeman, Vic Fulford, Mark Jones, Jeff Justice, Loren Lentz, Robert Manning, Alan Moore, Steve Moore, Brett Peacon,

George Peacon, Mark Reese, Tim Shirley, Marvin Sloan, David Smith, Steve Stevenson, Glen Woods, and Rick Wynn. Many of these gentlemen have been part of the team for more than a decade. They have traveled extensively to harvest deer, collect data, and implement habitat-improvement projects. Their professionalism has always made us proud. However, their most valuable contributions have been the observations and discussions they shared. The conversations about deer and deer management during the hundreds of nights we've spent in hotels, camps, and the back of trucks have truly furthered our education.

Our deer-management experience was made possible by clients who have trusted us with their wildlife resources for many, many years. These projects were frequently deer-management islands. That is to say these clients initiated site-specific deer-management programs before they were popular. They frequently suffered harsh criticism from neighbors and friends during the initial stages of their projects. Thankfully, they stayed the course, and in many cases became deer-management leaders in their areas. They provided us magnificent opportunities to apply our knowledge and refine our management techniques. To our valued clients, **thank you**.

Woods and Associates team members have spent many hours listening and sharing opinions on internet talk forums, especially on *www.tndeer.com*. Our thanks to the hundreds of participants who have shared our passion for the white-tailed deer and kept us sharp with their astute questions.

This is a book by Woods and Associates personnel about principles of deer-herd management and our beliefs about how deer herds work. This information is based on research and management projects that began in 1986 and have taken our team to properties throughout the whitetail's range.

About the Authors

All of the authors of this book are members of the Woods and Associates, Inc. (WAI) team, which was incorporated in 1990. WAI is one of the most experienced private wildlife management consulting firms in America. They are active in research and management projects throughout the whitetail's range and specialize in maximizing herd and habitat potential on a site-specific basis. The team is currently involved in projects throughout the central and eastern sections of the U.S., in habitat as diverse as the South Texas Brush Country, the Everglades of South Florida, the Adirondack Mountains of New York, and just about everything in between.

Grant Woods: Dr. Grant Woods, founder of WAI, is a wildlife biologist who specializes in habitat management and white-tailed deer population dynamics. He schooled at Southwest Missouri State University, the University of Georgia, and Clemson University. However, he often says "my best schooling has occurred while in the woods." Grant was raised on a farm in the Missouri Ozarks. He grew up hunting and trapping rabbits. He and his father hunted the early deer seasons of the area.

Grant's passion for deer drove him to attend college. During three college summer breaks, Grant worked for the U.S. Bureau of Land Management in Nevada, where he studied mule deer winter habitat and fought wildfires. This was the beginning of his understanding of how critical habitat management is to deer populations. The subject for Grant's Master's thesis was scrape behavior of white-tailed deer. Dr. Lynn Robbins directed his research and gave him a long-enough leash to explore new techniques. These new techniques included using

Photo by Kent Hensley

Dr. Grant Woods

infrared-triggered cameras Grant helped design and pioneer. This was before these cameras were commercially available. He used these cameras to document the sex and age of deer using scrapes. Grant's work with scrapes led to his rub behavior research projects conducted under the guidance of Drs. Larry Marchinton and David Guynn. Again, both of these mentors gave Grant a long-enough leash to explore new techniques into deer research and management.

During his Ph.D. rub research, Grant began working with hunting clubs from New York to Missouri. It was while working with these clubs that Grant truly began to understand deer management. These clubs allowed Grant to create deer management programs that used harvest criteria and data collection above and beyond state regulations. These experiences helped shape Grant's understanding and philosophy of deer biology and the human dimensions associated with deer management.

Grant enjoyed working with deer herds and deer hunters so much that he never looked for any other type of job. And today he continues working with deer hunters and managing and/or researching deer herds. Grant's extensive research in habitat improvement was used to create BioLogic© food plot blends. His years of study of palatability, productivity, digestibility, and nutritional quality of deer forages were the cornerstone for creating these blends.

Bryan Kinkel: Currently residing in Nashville, Tennessee, Bryan is the team's digital mapping and Geographic Information System (GIS) specialist. Before joining the Woods and Associates team, Bryan used his Earth Science degrees in his work with the U.S. Census Bureau, where he helped build the world's largest and most complex GIS project, the Census Bureau's Decennial Census. Bryan now uses those skills in developing innovative new techniques for the use of GIS technology in studying deer behavior and for evaluating management practices.

Bryan's intense interest in white-tailed deer began at age 16, when a slug from his borrowed, weather-beaten 16-gauge shotgun found its mark-a beautiful 8-point buck-on his first deer hunt. Since that time, researching white-tailed deer and figuring out "what makes them tick" has been his

Bryan Kinkel

overriding passion in life. Even before he joined the WAI team, Bryan turned his family's west Tennessee hunting property into a testing ground for various herd and habitat management techniques. Bryan has also conducted long-term research to analyze how terrain and habitat influence where bucks make rubs, as well as how herd dynamics drive buck rubbing behavior. The results of this research have aided the team in developing habitat management techniques that produce more predictable buck movement patterns.

Robert Bennett: Robert hails from Arkansas and serves as Conservation Community Project Manger for the WAI team. Robert's degree is in geology, and he has traveled many parts of the country and the Middle East working as a geologist, archaeologist, photographer, videographer, and webmaster most of his professional career. He also worked extensively with soil scientists, biologists, and GIS specialists before joining WAI.

Robert discovered the excitement of the hunt when his Uncle, Bob Porterfield, put a challenge before him. When Robert was 12 years old, Uncle Bob purchased a single-shot 20-gauge and told him it would belong to him when he passed the hunter education course. Robert's parents were not hunters, but supported his interest in the outdoors. After Robert passed the course, Uncle Bob introduced him to the great sport of hunting. To this day, Robert is grateful to Uncle Bob for launching him into an exciting world that most likely would have passed him by had his uncle not taken the time and effort to plant the seed for his lifelong ambition. Most importantly, Robert realized that when parents are not the teachers or mentors of hunting, it is up to others to ensure that today's youths are introduced to and have the opportunity to experience the thrill of the hunt.

Robert has filmed, directed, and produced two videos in conjunction with the Quality Deer Management Association (QDMA): *Proven Techniques for Managing Your Deer Herd* and *Enhancing Habitat on Your Hunting Lands*. Robert is also the founding president of the Central Arkansas Branch of QDMA. He has volunteered extensively for the Central Arkansas Quail Unlimited Youth Hunt and has served as co-chairman of the 2002 Arkansas Outdoor Youth Day-at the time, the largest outdoor youth event in Arkansas history. Robert

Photo by Dr. Harry Jacobson

Robert Bennett

founded and managed two hunting clubs totaling 5,000 acres before joining the WAI team.

About the Book

The material in this book is a compilation of the best and most recent deer research, conducted by myriad wildlife scientists. A healthy dose of "real world" experience from more than 20 years of managing deer across their range has been used to round out the scientific knowledge.

The format of this book is the result of a Deer Management 101 training course Woods and Associates team members have been presenting and perfecting for more than a decade. It became obvious that we could present this deer management training to many more hunters through the written word than we could ever reach via individual presentations.

As Dr. Woods mentions in the opening paragraphs of this chapter, deer are now so common across the eastern two-thirds of the United States that *many wildlife managers and hunters take them for granted.* This book is intended for hunters and managers who do not take deer for granted. The material in this book was chosen to provide an up-to-date reference source for factors that influence deer herd health and population dynamics. This book is also intended to explain the most common deer management techniques.

Although education on deer dynamics and management is the primary emphasis of *Deer Management 101*, we also believe it is critical to remind hunters of their role as the real managers of today's deer herds. Every hunter who has had a deer in his or her sights and decided to release the arrow or pull the trigger has made a management decision to remove that deer from the herd. Just as importantly, every hunter who has decided not to release the arrow or pull the trigger has also made a management decision-to leave that animal in the herd. Each decision affects the health and productivity of that herd. Although wildlife agencies set seasons and bag limits, hunters are the true deer managers. They are the only ones who can implement management goals through selective use of their trigger fingers.

The primary goal of this book is to educate hunters. Educated hunters realize their important role in deer management and therefore make wise management decisions. We believe it is much better for the sport of hunting to educate ourselves and other hunters than to have those who truly don't enjoy whitetails legislate deer management techniques. Hunters should understand that their activity can benefit society by limiting crop damage, deer-car accidents, and disease concerns. These "benefits to society" help preserve our hunting heritage. But enough about us and why we wanted to write this book. On with the education!

Grant R. Woods, Ph.D.
Bryan Kinkel
Robert Bennett

Photo by George Barnett

Chapter 2

What Is Deer Management?

Regardless of where you hunt or what weapon you use, all deer hunters have one thing in common. You are deer managers! If you have ever harvested a deer you have participated in deer management.

When a hunter pulls the trigger, more is at stake than venison for the freezer. The number, sex ratio, and age of the deer harvested in an area, as well as the ones left to walk,

The average hunter is the true manager for most deer herds in the country.

determine herd characteristics the next season. Although four-legged predators, disease, and automobiles will take some deer, it is the hunter (the two-legged predator) who selectively removes deer from the environment. Just as importantly, it is also the hunter who has the opportunity to harvest a deer, yet passes it by.

Regardless of whether you hunt on public land, a small farm, or a large block of leased industrial timber land, at the moment of truth, the decisions made by you and others who hunt there help determine the quantity and quality of deer you will hunt in the future. Perhaps you would like more deer on your property. Perhaps you want a quality deer herd more in

To shoot or not to shoot. Making intelligent decisions is the key to successful deer management programs.

Photo by George Barnett

Although deer are taken by natural mortality, it is the deer hunter who selectively removes deer from the environment.

Photo by George Barnett

This buck needs age and adaquate nutrition in order to reach his full potential.

tune with habitat conditions. Perhaps you even want to manage for trophy bucks on your hunting land. Regardless of your goals, the trigger finger or bow release is the key that opens the door to a successful deer management program. However, many other factors should be considered.

Deer management, just like business management, will have its successes and failures. Each management program has specific goals, property size limitations, a certain number of participants, constraints on available resources, and a plan to accomplish these goals. Those who correctly manage all of

Photo by George Barnett

With proper herd and habitat management, a buck like this can exist on any property in the country.

these factors are the ones who will enjoy the fruits of their labor. However, simply saying, "We are participating in a deer management program," will not yield a farm or forest full of large-bodied whitetails with trophy racks. Specific, well-designed guidelines must be followed to produce desired results.

Many deer hunters have preconceptions about deer management and how it works. Outdoor television shows, magazine articles, pictures on hunting products and pallets of deer corn have inundated today's deer hunter with notions of quick fixes. A supplemental feeding program, such as the extensive use of corn feeders, will not by itself yield a healthy herd and large bucks. We are familiar with a property in New York that once fed tons of corn every winter, yet the performance of the deer herd was poor. Body weights were extremely low, and

Photo by George Barnett

As long as your goals are matched with your resources, most obstacles to a deer management program can be managed.

reproductive success, or fawn survival, was terrible. On this property, for every 20 adult does, only one fawn was produced each year.

Many factors affect the results of a deer management program. For example, depending on the size of the land you manage, the management practices on adjacent properties certainly can affect the results of your program. Just as importantly, the type and condition of the habitat, and especially the food sources available, greatly affect your plan. Even weather conditions can have major impacts. However, as long as your goals are matched with your resources, most obstacles to a deer management program can be managed.

A sound and practical management plan, one that will give you the most bang for your buck, must take into account three major characteristics of a whitetail population:

1) adult sex ratio
2) age structure
3) herd density (the number of deer) and its relationship to the habitat.

However, to truly understand how deer management works in the present, you must first know its intriguing history.

Photo by George Barnett

Chapter 3

The History of Deer Management in North America

Little is known about white-tailed deer populations across North America before Europeans arrived. Populations were probably robust in areas with abundant grasslands and savannahs. Even in areas of mature forest, isolated weather events such as severe storms, ice storms and lightning-induced fires annually removed small to large sections of mature trees. These damaged or destroyed areas of timber would then regrow through the forest regeneration cycle. The first plants to appear during regeneration are weeds and grasses. Within a few years, weeds and grasses are replaced by brush. Eventually, the brush is replaced by saplings, and later by timber. The final stage of regrowth is a return to mature timber. Scientists refer to this habitat regeneration as "successional regrowth."

Deer populations found favorable habitat within the mosaic of young, medium, and mature forests that stretched from the Atlantic westward to beyond the Mississippi River, as well as in the patches of savannah and prairie scattered across eastern North America. With areas in the earliest stages of successional regrowth producing many low-growing food plants and subsequent stages providing excellent bedding cover, it appears that conditions favored a strong deer population across eastern North America. This assumption matches early European descriptions made during the 17th and 18th centuries.

Natural events such as severe storms and fires annually removed small to large sections of mature trees.

Natural openings in the mature forest canopy allow browse to grow within the reach of deer, and also provide bedding areas and escape cover that deer need to thrive.

The First Deer Managers

The impact of humans on deer populations has been negative and positive, and range from direct predation to extensive habitat modification. Human impacts have been as minor as harvesting a doe to feed a family, and as significant as eliminating entire deer populations and the habitat they occupy.

Climatic conditions and their associated environmental consequences were not the only factors strongly influencing the Pre-European settlement deer population. Archaeological evidence indicates the earliest human populations in North America focused their subsistence on killing large mammals. In fact, deer bones-including teeth and antler fragments-are common artifacts found in most archaeological deposits, such as bluff shelters and caves.

Archaeologists have investigated hundreds of Native American sites within major river valleys, as well as thousands of smaller upland cluster sites consisting of discarded stone artifacts. This is often interpreted as a cycle of gathering and dispersing of human groups as they refined hunting and gathering strategies. Large quantities of deer remains found at the larger sites attest to the importance of deer as an economic resource. Butcher marks on these bones provide archaeologists detailed information about procurement strategies and butchering techniques used during this period. Moreover, tools such as deer-bone awls used for sewing, antler-tine tools used for finishing spear points, and bone or antler tines used for projectile points demonstrate how deeply deer were imbedded in the Native American economy. Fragments of deer hide used for clothes, moccasins, and carrying pouches are also common finds.

Photo by George Barnett

Native American dart points such as this one were used to harvest deer before prehistoric bow and arrow technology was developed.

Not only were deer products used for food and tool-making, but various Native American groups also began a wide spread industry of deer-hide trading. Another example of deer being used for more than utilitarian purposes was found during the excavation of a ceremonial mound site used by the Caddoan confederacy-Native American tribes who occupied the four-states area of Arkansas, Texas, Louisiana, and Oklahoma. At this site in the Red River valley of southwestern Arkansas, investigators recovered a large cache of deer antlers. The cache, apparently stockpiled in a back room of this ceremonial structure, consisted of 2,042 skull plates and attached antlers. The investigators estimated that more than one-third of the original cache had been lost through impacts from modern agricultural activity, meaning the original cache may have contained more than 3,000 sets of antlers. This large collection clearly indicates the cultural importance of deer to the Caddo peoples.

Information about the way Native Americans and deer populations interacted before the 1500s must be derived solely from archaeology. Following European settlement, written narratives appear, and often describe Native American lifestyles and hunting practices.

It appears Native American groups not only used organized deer hunts far from their villages, but also used large-scale management techniques to increase the effectiveness of their hunting trips. These management practices included fire, particularly within forest openings and prairies. These periodic

Photo by John D. Northrip

Deer bones, antlers, and even hide have been recovered from Native American archeological excavations within the whitetail's native range.

Photo by John D. Northrip

Deer bones and mussel shells discovered in this bluff shelter midden in Northwest Arkansas provide clues to the past.

burnings produced abundant browse and thus more animals frequented the burned areas. This activity appears to have been so widespread that much of what is now the southeastern United States became a "pyrophytic" habitat-that is, habitat that requires or is enhanced by regular burning.

The Demise of Deer

The arrival of Europeans had disastrous consequences for the American Indian and the pyrophytic habitat they maintained. Native American populations plummeted because of famine and diseases introduced by Europeans. Along with the decline in Native Americans, the widespread use of fire as a habitat management tool also declined. Large pyrophytic habitats disappeared, such as the Southeast's longleaf pine forests and open grasslands. Not only did these habitats disappear, but so did vast amounts of nutritious, low-growing forage for deer, which this habitat produced.

Like the Native Americans, Europeans changed the landscape, although more significantly than did their predecessors. As the Euro-American populations grew and moved westward, they cleared forests for farmland and they cut timber to supply the growing need for building materials and firewood. Initially, the small farm lots they created were excellent deer habitat, although the ensuing complete forest removal reduced the deer habitat in large sections of the Eastern United States. At the same time, subsistence hunting with improved weaponry flourished, as did the fur trade. The combination of habitat loss and overwhelming harvest that resulted from market hunting began the dramatic decline of white-tailed deer in North America.

In the late 1800s, the development of railroads, and especially the invention of refrigerated boxcars, opened the door to the exploitation of deer through commercial market hunting. Venison and hides were shipped by rail to growing cities along the East Coast. As the market grew for these products, so did the exploitation. Records show that hundreds of tons of venison were imported annually to large cities.

Commercial market hunters used any means possible to kill deer. "Jack lighting," baiting, and other methods were used on a massive scale throughout the whitetail's range. The writing was on the wall, and deer numbers plunged because of market hunting. Eventually, no whitetails remained in large sections of their original range. State regulatory agencies

Photo Courtesy of Mrs. Jack Branch

Heavy meat poles such as this were common during the early market hunting era.

eventually outlawed market hunting, but it was too late for many regions of the country. The white-tailed deer had been wiped from the landscape.

The surviving deer herds were confined to remote swamps, steep mountains, and other areas that discouraged human habitation and were inaccessible to market hunters. Fortunately, these wild, isolated areas saved the white-tailed deer from destruction.

First Conservation Efforts

The first deer-restoration efforts began during the early 1900s. Whitetails from remnant populations were trapped and relocated to large private or public landholdings. Although most of these restocking efforts were conducted by state wildlife agencies, some of their efforts were never recorded. In addition, private individuals also conducted restocking efforts, but they rarely recorded or published records of their work. Exactly how many deer were restocked, where they were restocked, and where they came from will likely never be known. However, the actions of state agencies and determined individuals are the cornerstones of the whitetail herds we pursue today. Once small pockets of deer were transplanted, their populations grew and eventually mixed with other isolated deer populations. With protection from market hunting, these populations expanded rapidly, and eventually deer herds were restored across virtually all of the whitetail's historic range.

First Hunting Seasons

As deer populations continued to grow, state game agencies implemented limited hunting. Those participating in these early deer seasons were some of the only hunters to ever hunt "natural" deer herds. We define "natural" as herds where the adult sex ratio and age structure were not determined by hunting regulations. Rather, these herd characteristics were determined by habitat conditions and predation (four- and two-legged predators). These small deer herds had all the characteristics of healthy herds, including mature bucks, balanced adult sex ratios, and low herd densities. (All of these traits are critical components of a balanced deer herd, concepts we discuss in detail in Section II of this book.) These early seasons produced a hunting experience similar to what is produced by today's Quality Deer Management (QDM) practices.

Photo by George Barnett

Once small pockets of deer were transplanted, their populations grew and eventually mixed with other isolated deer populations.

Black-and-white photographs from those first seasons show hunters standing around meat poles sagging with thick-bodied, large-racked bucks. Those old, dog-eared pictures present a stark contrast to many of today's photos-color shots of hunters with small-antlered, small-bodied immature deer. The decline in buck quality from the "good ol' days" to the present is not because of poor deer genetics or inbreeding. Today, there are simply fewer mature bucks roaming many regions of the country. In addition, many regions are overpopulated with whitetails. Simply put, too many mouths are competing for limited food sources. Past hunting practices, such as buck-only harvests, have so skewed the adult sex ratio in many of today's deer herds that deer populations are primarily made up of old females and a few young males.

Modern Deer Management

During the last several decades, opportunities to harvest a deer have increased dramatically. As a result, many hunters have tired of simply filling their bag limit. Today, legions of sportsmen and women seek innovative and hands-on ways to play a larger role in managing deer on their properties. Rather than accepting the quality of the deer herd as a by-product of agency management guidelines, hunters have begun to design and implement management plans with *specific* goals and objectives for *specific* properties.

The trend toward active and thoughtful participation in deer management is on and it will continue to grow. Unfortunately, little solid information has been published outside of scientific literature to explain the three basic deer management strategies available to sportsmen, and the biological ramifications and hunting experiences associated with each program. We cover these topics in depth in chapters 7, 8 and 9.

Let's first look at the aspects of a deer herd hunters can actually change. We call these the "manageable characteristics" of a white-tailed deer herd. If hunters are intent on implementing an effective deer-management plan on the lands they hunt, they need to understand these characteristics.

Photo by George Barnett

Chapter 4

Adult Sex Ratio

The world of the whitetail is dynamic. On any property at any time, disease, social stress, and the availability of quality habitat all play major roles in the deer herd's health. Many characteristics determine the health of a deer herd, but only three can be practically managed by hunters:

1) adult sex ratio
2) age structure
3) density of the herd as it relates to its habitat

Photo by George Barnett

The three manageable characteristics of a deer herd include the adult sex ratio, the age structure, and herd density.

These three characteristics are primarily controlled by one thing: your trigger finger releasing an arrow or firing pin. In other words, hunter harvest controls the adult sex ratio, age structure, and herd density.

Deer mortality from auto accidents, disease, old age, predation, or any other natural cause is usually independent of sex. Therefore, hunter harvest-the trigger finger-is the main controlling factor of herd composition. Sportsmen control which deer are removed from the herd each season by making conscious decisions whether to shoot the animal when an opportunity exists.

The adult sex ratio is a prime example of a "manageable" herd characteristic. When we refer to the adult sex ratio

Photo by George Barnett

Road kill and natural mortality are usually independent of sex. Mortality by hunters is the only way to control deer herd composition.

of a whitetail herd, it is the ratio of does and bucks one year old or older. Fawns are not included in the calculations. So, what sex ratio should you strive for on a property? That depends on your management goals. As a starting point, let's examine the adult sex ratio of deer herds before Europeans began altering herd and habitat conditions in North America.

Natural Adult Sex Ratios

Biologists can study "natural" or normal herd sex ratios by researching whitetails at unhunted areas where predators such as bears, coyotes, and bobcats are their only threats. One such area is a large private property in Georgia where the WAI team has had a research project for six years. Located within two hours of Atlanta, this 7,300-acre parcel had not been legally hunted for nine years before our team began its research. Considering that wild deer rarely live longer than eight to 10 years, most of the herd on this property had "rolled over" or been completely replaced since the area was last hunted. Our study concluded that the adult sex ratio of this deer population was one buck for every 1.3 does-virtually a balanced adult sex ratio.

Several studies suggest a deer herd will have approximately one adult buck for every adult doe when hunting seasons don't influence the herd's sex ratio. Why is this important? A balanced adult sex ratio plays an important role in herd health by keeping competition for breeding rights high among bucks. Competition for breeding rights assures that enough bucks are available to breed most does during their first estrous cycle. When this occurs, the rut is short and intense (and very fun to hunt!).

Benefits of a Short Rut

In a short rut, nearly all does are bred within a four- to five-week period. Our study of the unhunted deer herd in Georgia found 95 percent of the does were bred within a four-week period. However, not all of the breeding was spread evenly across that four-week window. In most cases a peak in breeding lasts around 10 days. During this 10-day peak, 50 to 60 percent of all does will be bred. This peak in breeding is what most hunters call the "peak of the rut," when bucks are actively pursuing, or "dogging," does.

Unfortunately, with the unbalanced adult sex ratios that favor does now common across the whitetail's range, many hunters never see this classic "peak of the rut." Instead, they experience what we call a "trickle rut" where sightings of bucks

Photo by George Barnett

When the adult sex ratio is balanced, the rut is short and intense.

pursuing estrous does are rare, and these infrequent sightings are spread across several months in fall and winter. When adult does far outnumber adult bucks, many does will not be bred during their first estrous cycle. An individual doe is only in estrus-receptive for breeding-for a short time, approximately 24 to 48 hours. If the few bucks in the herd are off tending other does during those 48 hours, the opportunity is missed, and that doe will not cycle back into estrus until 28 to 30 days later.

In herds with many more does than bucks, some does may have to cycle in and out of estrus two or three times before being bred. At one of our projects in the Adirondack Mountains of New York, heavily unbalanced sex ratios produced a breeding season lasting 110 days before all does were bred. In fact the range of breeding dates was probably longer. We harvested only 20 does and checked the age of fetuses to determine this range, so it is doubtful our sample included the earliest or latest bred doe. In effect, that rut lasted nearly four months-a real trickle rut. The adult sex ratio observed by hunters at this club was 1 adult buck to every 9 adult does-the result of 20-plus years of intensive buck-only harvest.

A long, strung-out rut can cause other problems. In fact, keeping the rut short is important for many reasons. First, a short rut is less stressful on bucks. Chasing does and fending off aggressive rivals causes bucks to burn considerable body reserves. Even when the sex ratio is balanced, bucks can lose substantial weight during the breeding season. Researchers at different universities have noticed that even with a balanced adult sex ratio, unlimited quality feed, and a relatively small confined area, bucks may lose 30 percent of their body weight

Photo by George Barnett

Does that are not initially bred must wait 28-30 days before they come back into estrus.

from the stress of rutting activities. Imagine the body resources burned over a long, strung-out rut.

The longer the rut drags on the more winter fat reserves bucks must burn to meet their bodily requirements. Bucks spend much of late summer and fall building up these critical fat reserves. All of the fat reserves deer use to survive winter are typically acquired before brutal weather arrives. If winter food resources are limited, bucks run down from a long rutting season are at high risk of winter mortality from malnutrition, which usually leads to disease and/or predation.

A rut-weakened buck must also spend much of the following spring green-up, when food is abundant and most nutritious, rebuilding lost body weight instead of putting on new

Photo by George Barnett

A buck that goes through a trickle rut will lose most of his fat reserves prior to the stressful winter season.

muscle and bone tissue or growing new antlers. In essence, a rut-stressed buck may use all of the food resources he consumes during spring to replace what was lost during the previous winter, instead of using those food resources to grow a bigger body and larger antlers. A buck that enters the prime food production months of spring in a malnourished condition will never express (grow) his maximum genetic potential body size or antlers.

An unbalanced adult sex ratio that favors does allows yearling and even 2½-year-old bucks to participate in the rut. This activity consumes huge amounts of energy. When immature bucks expend this energy, it is taken from resources that could have been used for body and antler development. In addition, immature bucks can receive damaging or lethal injuries during the rut. When a dominance hierarchy is established as a

Photo by George Barnett

A buck entering spring green up that has to play "catch up" to replentish body reserves will never reach his full antler potential.

Photo by George Barnett

Young bucks that participate in the rut lose reserves that could be used for future body and antler development.

result of a herd with an older buck age structure, immature bucks are usually suppressed from fighting or breeding by dominance displays from mature bucks. Actual fighting among immature bucks is limited. This is why many deer breeders place a mature buck in their pens with several immature bucks.

Simply put, the older buck's presence keeps young bucks healthier and safer, because they do not unnecessarily expend body resources participating in the rut or burning resources to heal wounds from fighting. In the wild, young bucks living in a herd with mature bucks and a balanced adult sex ratio have a much better chance of expressing their full genetic potential later in life.

A long rut has other negative effects on a herd. A strung-out rut means a strung-out fawning season the following spring and summer. (Remember that a whitetail's gestation period is about 200 days.) If predators are abundant in an area, the timing of this fawn drop is critical. Coyotes, dogs, bobcats, bears and other critters prey on newborn fawns. During its first four to six weeks of life, a fawn's natural instinct is to lie still when approached by a predator and use its natural camouflage for protection. After six weeks or so, fawns are up and traveling with their mother and flee at a predator's approach.

When all does in a herd breed within a short time frame, say four to six weeks, the fawns are naturally dropped within a short time frame. This burst of fawning means predators have only a short time to find newborn deer. In this situation, which is called "prey saturation," predators can only catch a small percentage of the total fawn crop before the young deer are old enough to escape by fleeing.

However, if the whitetail's breeding season is strung out over several months, then fawns are born over several months. If this occurs, predators can take a heavy toll on the fawn crop. In short, an extended rut causes an extended fawning period, and an extended fawning period can increase predation on newborn deer.

A short, properly timed rut means most birthing falls into the latter stages of the spring green-up, when food

Photo by George Barnett

Predation is greatly increased when a trickle rut strings out birth dates through late summer and early fall.

resources are at their peak. This gives does ample food for producing milk and gives fawns the longest possible growing time before their first winter. This is the best scenario for a fawn crop to achieve maximum survival and growth rates. Fawns born late in the birthing season have limited time to grow before winter. In Northern states this can be critical. Unless fawns weigh at least 60 pounds by late fall, their chances of surviving harsh winters are very low. Even in the South where the climate is milder, late-born fawns will be smaller and less healthy than fawns born at the appropriate time. Some research indicates late-born fawns may require three to four years to catch up in antler growth with their earlier-born siblings, and may *never* catch up in body growth.

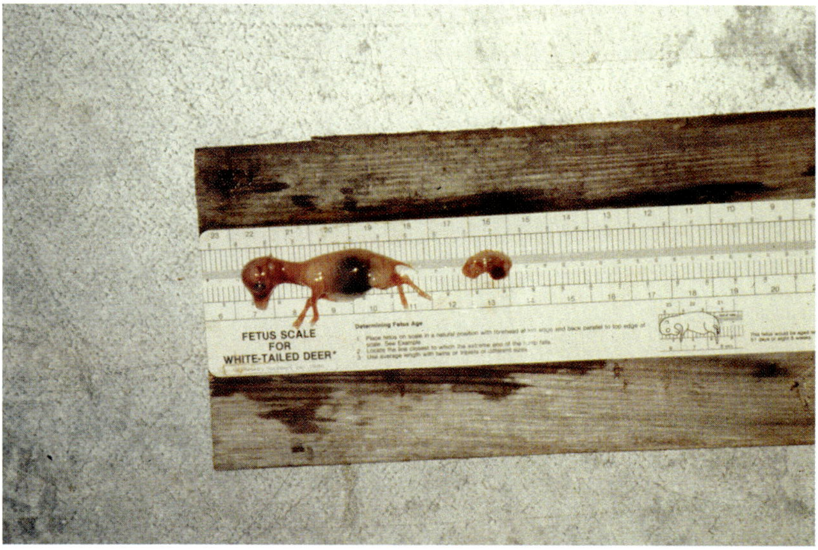

These fetuses are examples of different breeding dates on the same property.

Photo by Joe Hamilton

These male fawns had very different birth dates. Which do you believe has the best chance of expressing its potential?

Looking at this from the human angle, scientists have recognized for many years that nutrition during the first years of a child's life is critical to future mental and physical development. This is probably also true of most mammals, including white-tailed deer.

Managing the Sex Ratio of Whitetails

Managing the deer herd on your property to produce a balanced adult sex ratio can be very challenging. First is the ratio of adult bucks and does at the initiation of the management project. In a highly skewed situation, typically toward does, several years of selective harvests may be required to produce significant changes in a herd's adult sex composition.

Photo by George Barnett

If adult sex ratios are heavily skewed towards does, it may take several years of "trigger finger management" to bring ratios closer.

Learning to overcome tradition is another factor. For many years hunters were taught to shoot bucks and to pass up does. Does were considered the future buck producers and, in essence, became protected animals. Passed down from one generation to the next, the "protect a doe at all costs" philosophy became ingrained in our hunting ethics. It wasn't long ago that most hunters would no more shoot a doe than they would shoot their dog.

Although helpful in restoring deer herds in the early to mid 1900s, the common practice of shooting bucks and passing does placed heavy harvest pressure on buck populations in many parts of the country. Strict adherence to this "never shoot a doe" philosophy, often through several generations of hunters, caused severely out-of-balance deer herds. For example, in many Northern states, buck-only hunting is a longstanding tradition. Our research on several hunting clubs in the Adirondack Mountains of New York revealed a sex ratio of nine adult does for every adult buck!

Numbers like that dispute an oft-repeated mantra that it is physically impossible for the sex ratio of a whitetail herd to be worse than three does for every adult buck. But in many cases, this 3:1 ratio is calculated using large fawn crops in the calculations. With a typical 1:1 birth sex ratio (one buck born for every doe born) fawn numbers swamp the skewed adult sex ratio, causing the herd to appear relatively balanced. But fawns should *not* be included in adult sex-ratio calculations. Not only do these false calculations include fawns, but they also assume there will be large fawn crops each year to swamp the adult population's skewed sex ratio. But large fawn crops are not a given, especially in herds with unbalanced adult sex ratios that favor does. In such herds, fawn survival may be very low. We discuss fawn production in greater detail in the Herd Density chapter.

The Social Factor

If you are a deer hunter, you probably want to see big bucks. Even archaeologists have remarked that early cave drawings depict large animals with big horns and antlers. Apparently, large antlers have fascinated humans for eons. Today's outdoor media inundate hunters with images of big bucks, thus putting a lot of social pressure on them. But in most cases, bucks like seen on TV or in magazines don't exist on most hunting properties. Our natural desire to harvest bucks, combined with the media's obsession with big antlers, drive many hunters to believe that harvesting any buck, regardless of size, is better than not harvesting a buck at all. This "buck mentality," coupled with traditional buck-only harvest strategies, are two primary social barriers to managing deer herd sex ratios.

For example, hundreds of big-buck contests are held across America each year. When was the last time you entered a contest where a "big doe" yielded the best prize? Outdoor television shows and the amazing number of hunting videos on the market focus on killing "monster bucks." It is rare to see a doe harvested on film. Also, articles and advertisements in hunting magazines are geared toward helping hunters shoot big bucks. Never do you see an ad that reads, "This product will help you tag more does." Therefore, harvesting does is not something that excites hunters, and in some areas is still frowned upon.

Harvesting does is an essential part of almost all successful deer management programs.

Then there is the "machismo" of some hunters who believe it is not manly to shoot a doe. Unfortunately, that kind of thinking prevents you from balancing the adult sex ratio. You and your hunting buddies must shoot does if you expect to implement a deer management program that improves the herd's quality. Does must be harvested to balance the adult sex ratio and allow the herd to express its potential.

You can use this machismo to your advantage when managing the actions of others and changing the mindset of those who refuse to shoot does. A "big doe" or an "old doe" contest helps stir up competition. If you hunt where does are overpopulated, compete to see who can harvest the most dressed poundage of does, within legal harvest guidelines, of course. You may find that many hunters will participate, particularly in areas with minimal doe harvests and few mature bucks to brag about on the meat pole. Competition can sometimes fuel desirable results.

In some cases, it may be up to you to educate hunters. Provide articles, books, and videos about deer management. Show them scientific data from whitetail researchers to rebut stories told at the campfire by old Uncle Charley. For in Uncle Charley's past, passing does was the correct thing to do in many regions. However, that practice now harms most deer herds. We strongly encourage deer managers (hunters) to consider herd conditions and the management objectives for the herd when deciding whether the next deer they harvest is a buck or doe.

Photo by George Barnett

Chapter 5

Age Structure

An appropriate age structure is crucial if a deer herd is to reach its potential. Before discussing a herd's age structures in detail, it is important to understand deer age-classes. Deer, like many other animal species, have a specific breeding season that occurs once per year. The timing of their breeding season is linked to appropriate birthing dates.

White-tailed deer have a gestation period (pregnancy) of approximately 200 days. The timing of their fall breeding season should be such that the later stages of fetal development and birth occur 200 days later during the height of food production-spring and early summer. During winter, when food sources are limited, deer fetuses grow slowly. Finding limited winter food sources is a matter of survival to the mother doe, and she often has few resources to spare for fetal development. However, in the last few months of pregnancy, fetal development rapidly accelerates. Fetal growth should coincide with the flush of new growth that occurs during spring green-up. Not only are foods growing most rapidly at this time, but they're also peaking in nutritional content and digestibility. The timing of the fall breeding season to produce births during the year's peak food-production period is critical to successful fawn production.

Because most fawns are born at approximately the same time each year, late spring and early summer, deer herds are comprised of age groups, or "cohorts" of deer. Individuals in each cohort are the same age, and each cohort is separated from

Photo by George Barnett

The age structure of your deer herd will affect their overall performance.

other cohorts by one-year intervals. Each cohort is called an "age-class." When managers and hunters discuss deer age-classes, they are referring to the age of each cohort during the hunting season. Hunters and managers assign deer to age-classes by analyzing tooth replacement and wear patterns. With hunting season occurring in most areas between September and January and deer births usually occurring in late spring, a fawn crop is approximately 6 months old when harvested. Although any individual fawn may range in age from a few months to 8 months when harvested, depending on harvest and birth dates, the entire age-class of fawns is considered to be 6 months old, or the half-year-old age-class.

Fawns that survive their first hunting season and live for a full year to reach their second hunting season, advance into the 1½-year-old, or "yearling" age-class. As deer survive each hunting season, they advance into older age-classes, each separated by one year, and are always listed at the half-year mark (2½, 3½, 4½, etc.)

Managing Age Structure

As with adult sex ratios, white-tailed deer age structures are managed with the trigger finger. Pulling the trigger

In some states, yearling males make up 80 percent of the legal buck harvest! This buck was still a few years away from showing his antler potential.

guarantees that animal will not survive to the next age-class. Of course, passing up a deer does not ensure it will survive until the next hunting season, either. Deer will be lost to accidents, auto collisions, disease, poaching, etc., each year. But harvesting a whitetail *absolutely* ensures that deer will *not* survive to the next fall. This is one of the few immutable laws of deer management-dead deer do not grow!

Although age structure is not complicated to manage-you pull the trigger or you don't-major adjustments to age structure can take years to accomplish. If many older does or bucks are lacking in a herd, hunters must pass up young deer for several years to meet those goals.

Proper Age Structure

As we discussed in Chapter 1, archaeological excavations reveal that Native Americans were large consumers of white-tailed deer. They used meat, hides, antlers, and bones for food, clothing, and tools. Unused portions of deer were thrown in middens-communal trash heaps. Where soil conditions and climate are favorable, and natural and manmade disturbance have not occurred, middens remain fairly intact. Hundreds of middens have been examined, and much has been learned about the Native Americans' harvest of deer.

Considering Native Americans were subsistence hunters (they killed to obtain food), they harvested whatever deer they could, regardless of whether that deer was a buck, doe, or fawn. When your life depends on harvesting animals, you are not picky about the sex or age of deer you kill. This form of subsistence harvesting produced a useful "random sample" of animals from the local population. This sample provides a window into the structure of white-tailed deer herds that existed before Europeans arrived. After collecting and categorizing more than 3,000 lower jaws from middens, archaeologists determined that early deer herds had an advanced age structure with deer of every age present, including very old deer. The graph in Figure 5-1 displays the percent of Native American harvested deer in each age-class.

We believe this sample of Native American harvested deer ages is representative of a natural herd age structure. In Chapter 4, we discussed a project of ours in west-central Georgia, in which we could study a deer herd unhunted by man. From this herd we acquired data on natural adult sex ratios. The

Photo by John D. Northrip

Native American middens provide clues to natural sex ratio in natural environments.

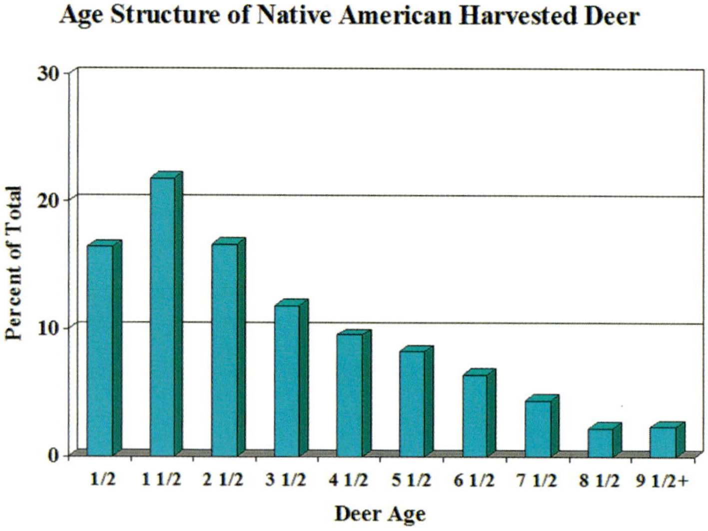

Figure 5-1. These data show the largest age-class of deer harvested by Native Americans was the 1½-year-olds (yearlings). Each older age-class (cohort) decreased in proportion of the total harvest. Several archaeologists believe the lower number of fawns in the sample is not representative of the harvest, but is because of the lack of "calcification" of fawn's bones, causing them to disintegrate. Notice the percentage of deer in the older age-classes, with deer 5½, 6½, and up to even 9½-plus years of age in the harvest.

first year we harvested deer from this herd also provided interesting information on the age structure of an unhunted herd. Our harvest data mirror the "random sampling" of Native American harvests. During this first harvest from the unhunted herd, hunters focused on harvesting adult females. This harvest scheme produced a fairly random sample of the doe population's age structure, illustrated in Figure 5-2.

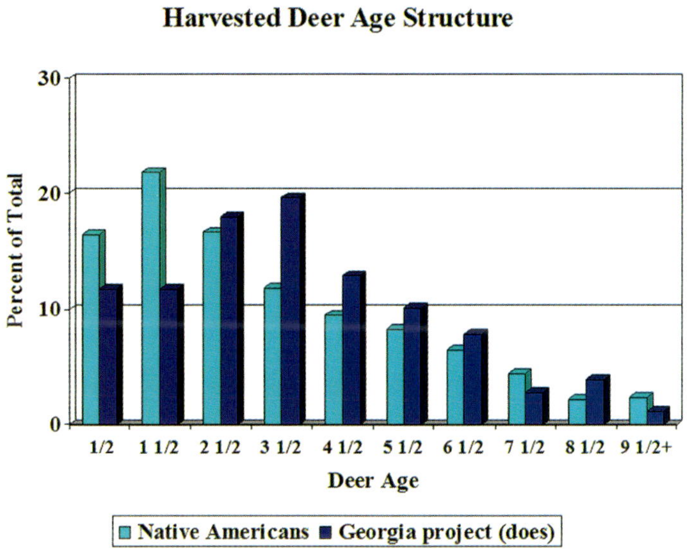

Figure 5-2. This graph depicts the age structure of Native American harvested deer compared to the harvest of female deer from a modern unhunted deer herd in Georgia. The two age structures look similar. We suspect the lower number of fawns, yearlings and 2½-year-old females in the Georgia harvest is caused by hunter bias. The hunters were attempting to harvest adult females and most likely harvested primarily large-bodied antlerless deer, reducing the harvest of the youngest and smallest-bodied antlerless deer (fawns through 2½-year-olds).

From the study of Native American harvested deer jawbones, scientists determined that in pre-European deer herds, 24 percent of deer were 5½ years old or older. In many regions today, deer herds contain adequate numbers of 5½-year-old or older does. But no state in the whitetail's range currently has a buck age structure statewide similar to herds before Columbus reached America. Because of traditional harvest guidelines, the

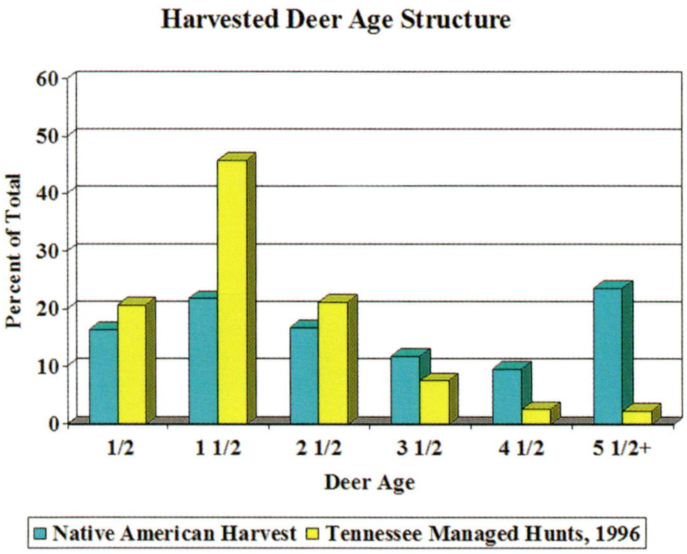

Figure 5-3. This graph displays the age structure of deer harvested by Native Americans compared to deer harvested on "managed" hunts (Wildlife Management Areas, Refuges, state-owned land, etc.) in Tennessee during 1996 hunting seasons. Deer harvested during the Tennessee managed hunts did not have as old of an age structure as deer harvested by Native Americans. A higher percentage of deer harvested in the Tennessee modern hunts were yearlings. This high harvest of young deer reduced the number of older deer in the herd. Yet this graph does not tell the whole story. A significant disparity in age structure existed between male and female deer in the Tennessee harvest. The Tennessee deer harvest is broken down by deer sex in Figure 5-4.

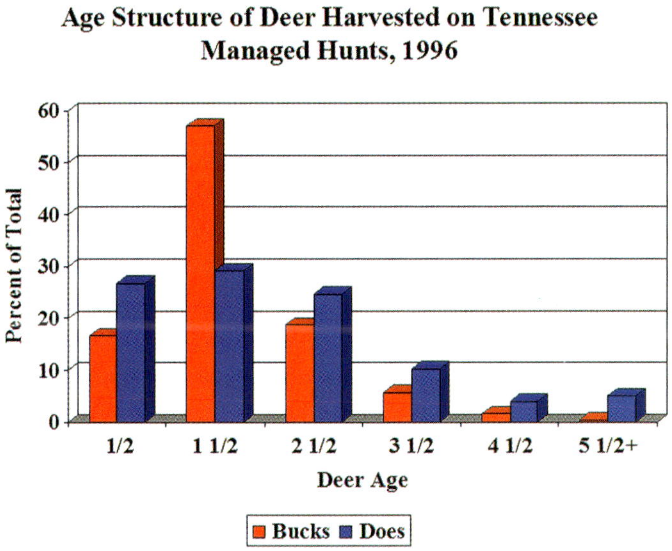

Figure 5-4. The age structure of deer harvested during 1996 Tennessee managed hunts displays the disparity between buck and doe age structures common across the whitetail's range. The harvested does were noticeably older than the harvested bucks. The percent of harvested female deer 5½ years old or older was 12 times higher than harvested male deer of the same age-classes. Why were there so few older bucks in the Tennessee harvests? Because bucks of those ages no longer existed. Nearly 60 percent of the Tennessee harvested bucks were yearlings (1½-year-olds), and many years of high yearling buck harvests prevented bucks from surviving to older age classes.

Note: Since Tennessee's wildlife agency reduced the buck bag limit in 1998, the age structure of harvested bucks across the state improved. At the writing of this book, yearling buck harvests have declined to nearly 50 percent, 2½-year-old bucks have increased to around 30 percent, and 3½-year-old and older bucks now comprise approximately 10 percent of the annual buck harvest. These numbers do not match a "natural" age structure, but are examples of how some state agencies have begun to address the problem of unnaturally low buck age structures.

buck segment of most herds has been overexploited. In fact, in some states, yearling males comprise 80 percent or more of the legal buck harvest. Although it is hard for many hunters to believe, in these high buck exploitation areas, hunters shoot nearly all of the yearling male age-class each year. Simply put, few bucks advance to the next age-class. Figures 5-3 and 5-4 display the age structure of harvested deer from modern hunts in Tennessee.

Because dead deer don't grow, the number of bucks that survive hunting season and advance into the next older age-class is extremely limited across much of the whitetail's range. This type of management, continued for generations of hunters, greatly suppresses the number of mature bucks in the population. In many regions and states, the number of bucks 3½-years old or older is less than 5 percent of the total buck population.

Another real-world example of low buck age structures can be found on our friend Dr. Larry Marchinton's property. Dr. Marchinton, a retired professor from the University of Georgia, directed one of the nation's most respected and progressive white-tailed deer research programs. During the 1970s and

1980s, Dr. Marchinton and his family managed deer on their land as most deer herds in the United States were managed at the time. This included harvesting all legal antlered bucks they observed. Legal bucks seldom survived a harvest opportunity.

The accompanying photo displays the antlers of all bucks killed on his property during a 15-year period. Each group represents bucks of a single age-class, and the antlers are arranged from smallest to largest within each age-class group. Notice the largest group on top. The bucks on this board are yearlings (1½-year-olds), and comprise most of the buck harvest. The bottom left board contains the 2½-year-old bucks harvested on the property during the same period. As you can see, there were far fewer 2½-year-old bucks harvested. The group on the bottom right shows the two 3½-year-old bucks harvested on the property.

This buck harvest represents the total bucks killed by four experienced hunters over a 15-year-period-or, in other words, 60 hunter years. In 60 hunter-years, only two 3½-year-old bucks and only nine 2½-year-old bucks were taken. The hunters killed *no* bucks older than 3½ years old. Why? Probably because no bucks older than 3½ years old existed on the property!

With the high harvest of yearlings, few antlered males survived their first hunting season. Of the few yearlings that saw the next season, few of those 2½-year-olds survived to the following year. Again, we emphasize that in 60 hunter-years, only two 3½-year-old bucks were killed, simply because they were so rare on this property. We believe this example looks familiar to most deer hunters.

Photo by Dr. Larry Marchinton

The antlers on top, bottom left, and bottom right boards are 1½-, 2½-, 3½-years old, respectively. Imagine how many racks could have been on the bottom left board if 1½- and 2½-year old bucks were passed!

Study the photos and notice the major increase in antler development between the age-classes. On average, the racks of the 2½-year-old bucks are much larger than antlers of the yearlings. In fact, in many areas the average 2½-year-old buck produces twice the antler growth as the average yearling buck. The two 3½-year-old bucks have considerably larger racks than the 2½-year-olds. However, as impressive as the 3½-year-old bucks are-most hunters would consider them exceptionally large bucks-they were not yet fully mature and had not reached their peak antler potential.

The bucks harvested from the Marchinton property were typical of a traditional management program. Most bucks killed are yearlings. Hunters occasionally shoot a 2½-year-old buck with a nice rack. The rare 3½-year-old buck is considered a "buck of a lifetime." It is a sad state of affairs when average-sized, not-yet-fully mature bucks are so rare they are deemed trophies. However, it is encouraging that with a proper harvest strategy, many of these younger bucks can move into the older age-classes. If you and the folks you hunt with have itchy trigger fingers, shoot the adult doe instead of the young buck. Improving the buck age structure can be that simple in most cases.

The Benefits of Proper Age Structure

Although few deer herds across the country currently have the proper buck age structure, older bucks are essential to the normal behavior of a deer herd. Fully mature bucks play a much greater role in herd performance than most hunters and

Photo by George Barnett

Mature bucks like this are few and far between throughout most of their range.

Photo by George Barnett

An ever-growing body of evidence indicates that older-age bucks produce "pheromones" that affect other deer.

managers realize. A growing body of evidence indicates older bucks produce pheromones that affect other deer. Pheromones are chemicals secreted from the producer's body that affect other animals. Once received (tasted, smelled, etc.), pheromones trigger special receptors. Pheromones can cause various changes in the receiving animal's physiology and behavior. The complexities of this social-biological interaction are not fully understood, but are believed to trigger production of specific hormones. How pheromone interactions work in white-tailed deer has not yet been proven, but the powerful influences pheromones play in other mammalian species have been well documented. Within the medical research community, pheromone production and influence are accepted processes of human biology.

Research suggests that primarily older bucks produce "controlling" pheromones. Yearling bucks are not physically mature enough to produce them. Some studies even suggest a buck reaching dominant status produces different pheromones than less dominant bucks of the same age. How the buck's body "knows" he has become dominant and begins producing "dominance" pheromones is not well understood, but is regulated by a system of internal messengers called hormones.

One effect of pheromone production by mature bucks is the timing of the rut. We've discussed how a balanced adult sex ratio reduces the length of the breeding season. New research suggests the presence of mature bucks may help keep breeding seasons tightly timed and may even cause the rut to occur earlier during fall.

Photo by George Peacon

Trigger finger management is needed in areas where the adult sex ratio is skewed towards does.

In some regions, such as the Southeastern U.S., the rut's advancement can be substantial. For example, we collected breeding season (fetal) data for 11 years from a project near Charleston, S.C. During this time, the harvest regime was designed to increase the ratio of bucks to does and increase the age structure of the buck population. We accomplished this by requiring each hunter to harvest four does before earning a buck tag. Buck harvests were limited to males, 3½-years old or older, using harvest criteria developed from data collected on-site. It is important to note these guidelines were self-imposed, not regulated by a state agency.

For those unfamiliar with seasons and bag limits in South Carolina, the rifle season for bucks during this project was open August 15 through January 1, with no daily bag limit. Doe harvests also were unlimited after September 15. To manage for mature bucks, hunters must be committed to not harvesting immature bucks when season length and bag limits are so liberal.

After we followed our harvest guidelines for seven years, the average date of breeding shifted 30 days earlier! Similar results have been produced on properties in Mississippi and New York, with peak average breeding dates shifting 10 to 30 days earlier once sex ratios were more balanced and buck age structures improved. Apparently, this shift in breeding dates was influenced by the increased density of older, dominant bucks. These dominant bucks produce the pheromones that cause does to enter estrus earlier than normal. Actually, "earlier than normal" is not quite right. In most locations,

By following a balanced harvest strategy, it is possible to develop a well-balanced age structure and sex ratio on your hunting property.

information on the "normal" timing of estrus has been gathered from deer herds with skewed adult sex ratios favoring does and few mature bucks. Simply stated, most researchers didn't begin collecting breeding date data until herds were exposed to many years of buck-only harvest. Data from herds with unbalanced adult sex ratios and an immature buck age structure probably represent an abnormal timing of estrus.

When sufficient mature bucks are present, the earlier estrus noticed in research projects is likely the true normal time for breeding. Therefore, it would be more accurate to say the presence of old bucks causes does to reach estrus at the normal time, while an absence of mature bucks causes does to undergo delayed estrus. With that said, a delayed rut is what most hunters are used to seeing, because buck age structures are fairly poor throughout most of the whitetail's range.

As we mentioned, earlier breeding dates mean fawns are born at the appropriate time in spring and early summer, giving them maximum growing time before winter. This, along with a shorter rut that reduces stress on bucks, is good for the deer herd's health. Again, we stress that by practicing harvest strategies intended to increase the buck age structure and balance the adult sex ratio, you are not participating in some "Frankenstein" process of creating giant, easy-to-harvest deer. You are simply following a practice intended to return herds to their normal breeding times and correct the late breeding created by many years of maximum buck harvest management. By following a harvest strategy designed to balance the adult sex ratio, it is possible to develop a well-balanced age structure and sex ratio on your hunting property. Just producing these

Photo by George Barnett

Within the whitetail's social structure, body size (not antler size) and aggressiveness usually drives the social status of bucks.

Young bucks that share their range with an older age class of bucks spend more time filling their reserves instead of losing them to the rigors of the rut.

seemingly minor changes can have profound positive effects on the health of the entire herd.

The Process of Subordination

The lack of older-aged bucks can produce additional concerns. Pheromones produced by older bucks likely induce or magnify the process of "subordination." Deer, like many other animals, have a complex social structure based on dominance and subordination.

Within the whitetail's social structure, body size (not antler size) and aggressiveness usually drive the social status of bucks. Generally, the healthiest, largest-bodied, and most aggressive bucks are the dominant animals in an area. Because older bucks are usually larger in body than younger bucks, they typically dominate. In a herd with a normal age structure, young bucks are too small to compete for dominant status. Thus young bucks must play a subordinate role.

It seems on the surface that the way dominant bucks are favored in the wild, that subordinate bucks would not receive any benefit from the dominance hierarchy. However, the subordination of young bucks may be good for them. Some researchers believe that by putting a dominant buck in close association with smaller or younger bucks, these lesser bucks experience a sudden decline in production of the male hormone testosterone. This testosterone reduction suppresses the subordinate bucks' aggressiveness, rut-related marking activities (rubbing and scraping), and most importantly, their desire to breed.

Suppressing sexual behavior can help young, subordinate bucks grow larger. Because their desire to breed is reduced, they spend less time participating in rutting activities like chasing, fighting and rut-marking. Instead of using valuable body resources during the rut, young bucks spend the fall feeding. Hence, they can put on additional weight and antler growth the following spring instead of replacing resources lost during the rut. By being forced out of the rut by the mere presence of older age-class bucks and their pheromones, subordinate bucks are not rut stressed, which allows them to express more of their growth potential. Young bucks receiving this growth opportunity have a much better chance of becoming larger bucks at maturity and more capable of becoming dominant. They wait their turn as intended and then become the large,

Photos by George Barnett

Competition resulting from an older age class of bucks ensures the healthiest deer pass on their genetic traits.

small bucks are not necessarily inferior bucks. They are most likely just young bucks.

The genetic makeup of an individual does not change with age. Again, this reinforces the importance of the domination/subordination process that takes place only in a herd with the presence of mature bucks. Competition between older bucks ensures the biggest, strongest, healthiest males become dominant and pass on their good genetics more often than subordinate bucks of the same age. These same-age bucks may have been subordinated because they did not have the genetic qualities chosen through natural selection-health, body size, and aggressiveness. In addition, young bucks without the opportunity to express their genetic potential are kept from breeding, and passing on unknown and unproven genetic qualities, through the subordination process. Natural processes can be complicated, but the processes of Natural Selection have fine-tuned a species over many generations to produce long-term benefits to the population.

Finally, it should be mentioned that some researchers believe does actually select their mates, although this has not been scientifically proven. In herds with a natural adult sex ratio and age structure, mature does may play a role in deciding which buck breeds them. If does do indeed play a role in choosing their mates, dominant bucks have a greater chance of passing their genes. The dominant does would allow only "acceptable" bucks to breed with them. Exactly what criteria does might use in selecting mates is unknown, but they would probably be linked to the health and social status of the bucks.

Signposting

Old bucks are responsible for an important type of rut sign known as the "signpost" rub. A signpost rub is a large-diameter tree that is rubbed by bucks year after year. Look closely at one of these big rubs and you'll see scarring on the tree from several years of rubbing. From our research, we believe signpost rubs play a critical role in the social dynamics of a deer herd.

Our observations suggest old-age bucks deposit pheromones on these signpost rubs. As mentioned, pheromones trigger the timing of estrus and play an important role in the dominance/subordination process. Although all deer interact with signposts-they will look at them, smell them, and touch them-only older bucks create them. Signpost rubs appear to be the primary location at which mature bucks leave their scent communications. In essence, the large rubbed trees act as communal pheromone wicks-or local bulletin boards.

Bucks using signpost rubs as communal pheromone wicks would explain why signposts are often found in locations with high deer traffic. Typically these large-diameter rubbed trees are located along a habitat or topographic feature that funnels deer from different social groups through a common area -for example, from a staging zone to a preferred feeding location.

We have also found a correlation between the number of rubs in a given area and the population of older bucks. This is especially true of signpost rubs. As the age structure of a buck population increases, so do the number of rubs and signpost rubs that appear each fall. On a project in western Tennessee, we monitored the changes in adult sex ratio and buck age

From our research, we feel signpost rubs play a critical role in the social dynamics of a deer herd.

structure as hunters implemented a harvest plan intended to improve these two herd factors. At the same time, we monitored the density and size of rubs on the property. As adult sex ratios became more balanced and the buck age structure improved, the number and size of rubbed trees increased dramatically. At the beginning of the project, rub densities were approximately 700 rubs per square mile (1.1 rubs per acre). Within five years of beginning the herd-improvement project, rub densities had increased to an amazing 5,000 rubs per square mile (7.8 rubs per acre). That is an increase of over 600 percent in just five years! Not only did the number of rubs increase dramatically, the size of rubbed trees also increased. For reference purposes, a 12-ounce aluminum soft-drink can is 2.6 inches in diameter. At the beginning of our project, we found no rubs on trees as large in diameter as a soft-drink can. By the sixth year of the project, the number of rubs on trees that size exceeded 300 per square mile!

Management Dilemmas

One common dilemma in managing the buck age structure is the "checkerboard" landownership patterns of modern America. Across the whitetail's range, large, contiguous single-owner properties are disappearing. These large landholdings are increasingly subdivided into smaller and smaller parcels. Properties of 100 to 250 acres are the norm in many areas.

From a management perspective, small lands are a problem because old bucks can have large home ranges. Depending on habitat conditions, fully mature bucks may cover several square miles during their daily travels, especially during the rut (although we believe the better the habitat, the smaller a buck's home range will be). It can be difficult to change the age structure of bucks on a small property when hunters on surrounding lands do not practice the same form of deer management.

As an example, if you and your hunting buddies pass up immature bucks on your property, they might walk across the property line and be harvested by hunters on adjoining land. This obviously hurts your ability to improve the buck age structure on your small tract. This is frustrating and often leads to hunters saying, "If I don't shoot that buck, somebody else will." As with most aspects of deer management, this problem can often be solved. Talk to your neighbors and let them know you are passing up young bucks on your property and explain

From a management perspective, small lands can be a problem because old bucks can have large home ranges. Yet, even this can be managed.

why. If your actions are sincere, you will likely find that other hunters will follow your lead.

It will take at least this level of effort to get the ball rolling. But once it starts rolling, it generally starts to snowball. This phenomenon can be linked to the growing number of states that have implemented antler restrictions. Whenever discussions turn toward hunters voluntarily protecting young bucks, a common comment we hear is, "That will never work in my area." Apparently, we must not have worked in "your area" yet. We have worked with herds throughout the whitetail's North American range and have been able to increase buck age structures on all of these projects. Protecting young bucks is more difficult in some areas than others. However, committed

Hunters across America that consistently pass up bucks like this are successful at moving more deer into the older age class on their property.

hunters willing to turn their property into an "island" of well-managed deer have consistently made a difference. Someone must set the example.

Real-world successes are often the quickest way to convince doubters. Don't hide your early successes while trying to increase the buck age structure. If you implement a management plan despite the fact your neighbors are not participating, show them your earliest success. Show them any older bucks you harvest to prove that passing up young bucks works. Pictures speak volumes! You can use trail cameras to photograph older bucks, and show those pictures to your neighbors. These pictures of older bucks in the area may convince them that passing up young bucks will not eliminate their chances of harvesting a buck. Leading by example and educating your neighbors is often the best way to persuade them to participate.

Another problem with managing buck age structures is the "I have to get my buck" syndrome. Many hunters seem to have a deep-seated need to harvest at least one buck each year, no matter its age or size. This is probably a function of peer pressure, because many hunters don't want to go home without antlers. If any hunter on a property thinks that way, you will have great difficulty improving the age structure of the bucks. We can't stress enough that dead deer don't grow!

Finally, many hunters are not confident when it comes to field-judging the age of bucks. This is not necessarily the hunter's fault, considering many hunters nationwide have little experience observing old-age bucks. During our workshops and seminars, we find most hunters can readily identify a mature doe because they have watched hundreds of mature does and fawns. They have elected not to harvest these animals and, as a result, had plenty of time to study them on the hoof. However, as soon as they observe an antlered buck, many hunters reach for the trigger, not the binoculars. We strongly suspect most deer hunters during their entire hunting career have spent less than 10 cumulative minutes observing mature bucks. As soon as they observe a mature buck, they start throwing lead or arrows.

However, given practice, hunters can easily judge the age of bucks. Body size, body shape, and antler development can help classify bucks into simple categories, such as young bucks, middle-aged bucks, and mature bucks. For management purposes, hunters can learn to separate yearlings from 2½-year-olds, 2½-year-olds from 3½-year-olds and so on. Once you learn to do that, you can start passing up immature bucks and improving the age structure of deer on your property.

It would be interesting if the directors of big-buck contests displayed the age of each buck showcased at their events. Hunters who go to these shows could study the mounted bucks and get a good feel for antler characteristics common to each age-class of buck. Many mounts displayed at shows are not "monster" deer; they are just older than most hunters observe while hunting. These large bucks may simply represent the average size of mature bucks in the area. When hunters see the size of truly mature bucks shot in their area, they may be inclined to start passing up younger bucks.

Buck age structure is one of the easiest herd characteristics to manage. It is simply management through trigger-finger control. Every time a hunter pulls the trigger, or elects to pass an opportunity to harvest a deer, that hunter has made a deer-management decision. Hunters are the herd managers, and the sooner they accept that role, the sooner they can begin to make wise management decisions.

Photo by George Barnett

Chapter 6

The Relationship of Herd Density to Herd and Habitat Quality

The third manageable characteristic of a deer herd is its density (deer per square mile), or total population. A close relationship exists between a herd's density and the herd's body weights, antler development, and reproductive capabilities. This relationship is driven by a habitat's ability to provide cover and produce quality forage. Throughout the whitetail's range, each local habitat can sustain a finite number of healthy deer. If too many deer inhabit an area, the habitat declines from over-browsing, and so does the herd's health.

When deer are consuming low quality forage, such as redcedar, the herd has obviously exceeded the habitat's capacity to produce quality foods.

Scientists often refer to "inverse" relationships. For example, consider two factors, "A" and "B." When factor A goes up it causes factor B to go down, which means factor A is inversely related to factor B. Herd density and herd quality are such an inverse relationship. When density increases, herd quality-the herd's overall health-decreases. In wildlife management, this is termed the "herd density to herd quality" relationship. Because the quality of a deer herd is inversely related to herd density, herd quality is "density dependent." In other words, the health and reproductive capabilities of a deer herd depend on the herd's density.

As mentioned, the herd density to quality relationship is driven by a habitat's ability to support deer. Hunters often forget that habitat quality also declines as deer numbers

Deer can and will literally eat themselves out of house and home if their numbers are not held in check, as evidenced by this woody browse that has been stripped down by deer.

increase. A particular habitat can produce only so much deer food. Eventually, a growing herd can eat itself out of house and home. This overbrowsing causes long-term damage to habitat. Deer are selective eaters, consuming the best resources first. In a high-density herd, deer may eliminate all top-choice food sources-perhaps permanently. In areas with high whitetail densities, where extensive browsing occurs for many years, ecologists worry that some plants may have become extinct.

Because increases in deer populations cause declines in the quality of a herd and the quality of the habitat, we expand the herd density to herd quality relationship to "herd density to herd and habitat quality" relationship. The quality of both the herd and habitat are inversely related to the herd's density, as displayed in the following graphs:

Herd Density to Herd and Habitat Quality

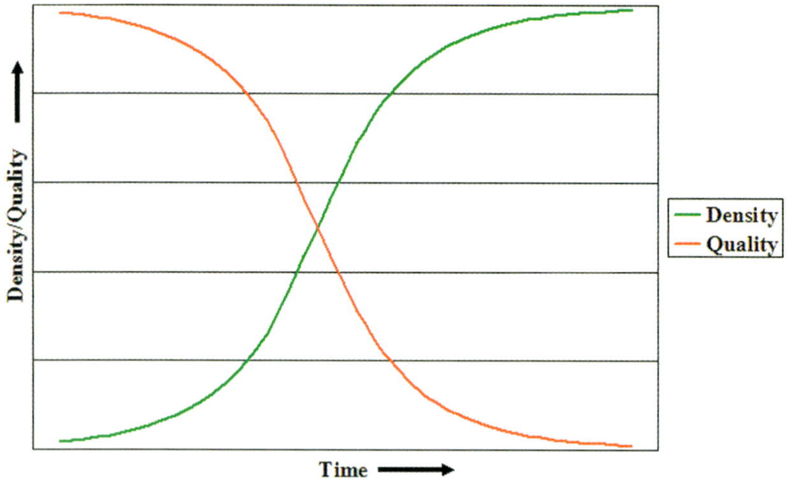

Figure 6-1. The above Herd Density to Herd and Habitat Quality graph is a hypothetical timeline that displays a deer herd's population growth. It also shows the relationship between herd size and the quality of deer and their habitat.

The horizontal scale (left to right) is time, with the far left of the graph representing an arbitrary point in time when a few deer are introduced into a habitat. As time passes (moves to the right along the graph), the deer herd increases through reproduction. The vertical scale represents the density of deer and the quality of the herd and the habitat, with the bottom of the graph being low values and the top of the graph being high values.

Notice that no exact numbers are used on the vertical scale. The exact values would be site-specific and could vary by location, depending on habitat condition and type. The graph's green line represents the number of deer in the herd or, more accurately, the deer density. The red line represents herd quality and habitat quality.

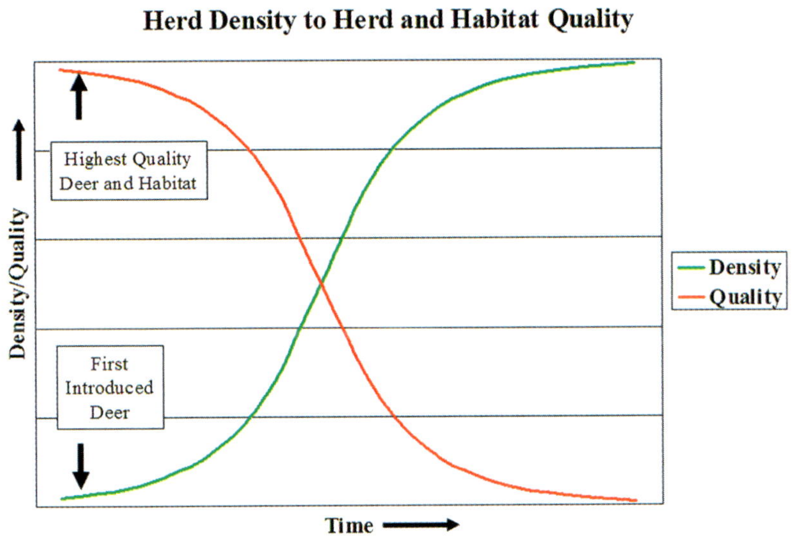

Figure 6-2. The far left of the graph depicts the starting point of a hypothetical herd. Imagine that a few deer are introduced into a habitat that contains no deer. At this point, the deer density (green line) is very low, and the quality of the herd and habitat (red line) are very high. Deer are scarce, and the habitat contains the maximum amount of high-quality deer feed. The health, body growth, antler development, and reproductive success (number of surviving fawns produced per doe) of the deer are at their peak.

Additionally, the low deer density precludes any negative social interactions among does and bucks. Therefore, reproductive success is maximized for the habitat. Given the high availability of nutritious food sources, each doe produces the largest number of fawns she can, and fawn survival is at its peak.

Habitat conditions and types play a major role in site-specific carrying capacities.

An open canopy provides forage as long as deer are kept within numbers the habitat can support .

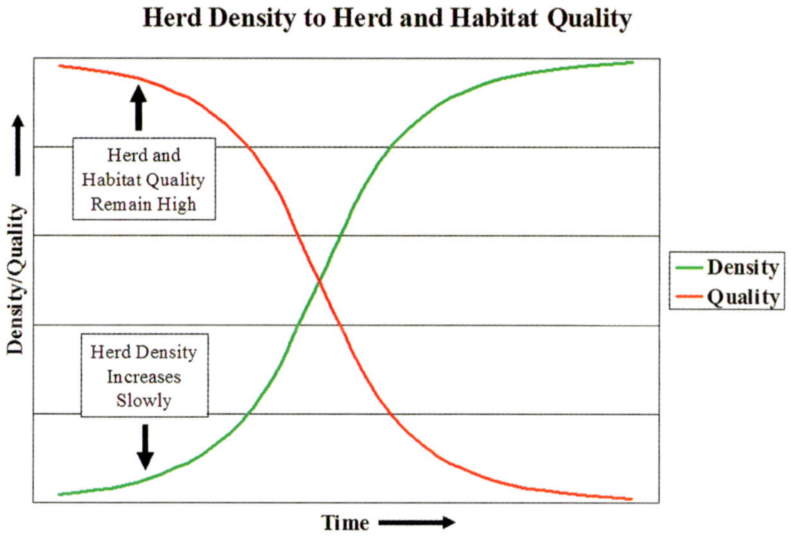

Figure 6-3. Notice as time advances herd density increases slowly. This is because of the small number of deer at the beginning of the experiment. Although deer are healthy and does are producing the largest number of surviving fawns per doe, the few does present can produce only so many total fawns. From year to year, the number of deer increases slowly. Inversely, the herd and habitat quality decline only slightly. The habitat still supports abundant top-quality food sources.

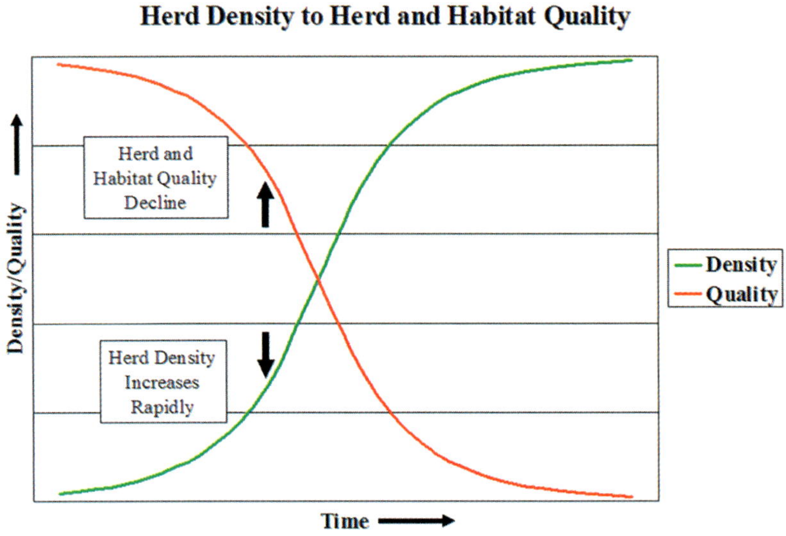

Figure 6-4. Moving farther along the timeline and to the right on the graph, the density begins to rise faster. The larger number of does in the population can produce a substantial fawn crop each year, rapidly increasing the total deer population. This process is very similar to compound interest rates. A small investment produces a small total return from year to year, but as the amount of the principal increases, so does the annual amount of interest earned.

On the other hand, notice how the quality of the herd and the habitat (red line) also begins a fast decline. The increasing deer population consumes more and more of the best foods. This leaves less high-quality food in the habitat to be shared among many more mouths. In this situation, a growing percentage of each deer's diet is made up of lesser quality foods. This growing reliance on poor foods produces declines in overall health.

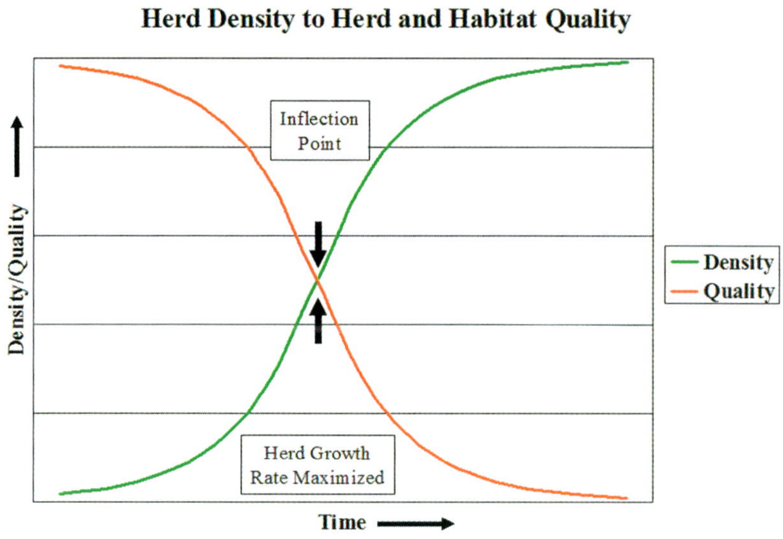

Figure 6-5. Now take a look at where the density curve (green line) changes directions. This change in curve direction, termed the "inflection point," is important for several reasons and will be mentioned often throughout the rest of this book.

At the inflection point, the herd's growth is at its maximum. Deer are increasing their numbers faster than at any other point in the process. Although the number of fawns produced per doe is not as high as it was earlier on the timeline (when the herd density was lower), many more does are producing fawns.

Photo by George Barnett

At the inflection point, the growth of the herd is at its maximum.

At the inflection point, deer are also increasing their numbers faster than at any other point in the process.

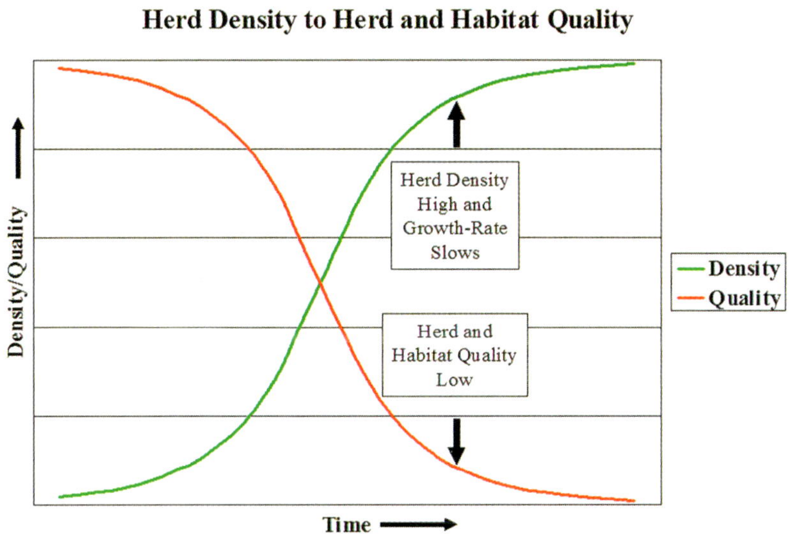

Figure 6-6. To the right of the inflection point, the herd's growth slows. Although the deer population has increased, the declining reproductive success of the does reduces the total number of fawns born and recruited into the herd each year. Most hunters assume that more does in a herd means more fawns produced each year, but that is not how deer population dynamics work.

As herd density rises rapidly, habitat quality declines rapidly. Beyond the inflection point, deer consume most, if not all, of the top food sources each year. Once the best feed is gone, a growing percentage of each deer's diet consists of second and third choice foods that are less nutritious.

When a growing number of whitetails are forced to eat less-nutritious foods, several things become noticeable. Deer body weights are not as heavy as when the herd was at a lower density. Bucks' antler development suffers, as does the reproductive success of does. There are more adult does in the herd, but they produce fewer fawns per doe than did the healthier does at lower densities.

Photo by George Barnett

When deer numbers exceed the carrying capacity of the habitat, nutritious forage is sometimes eliminated.

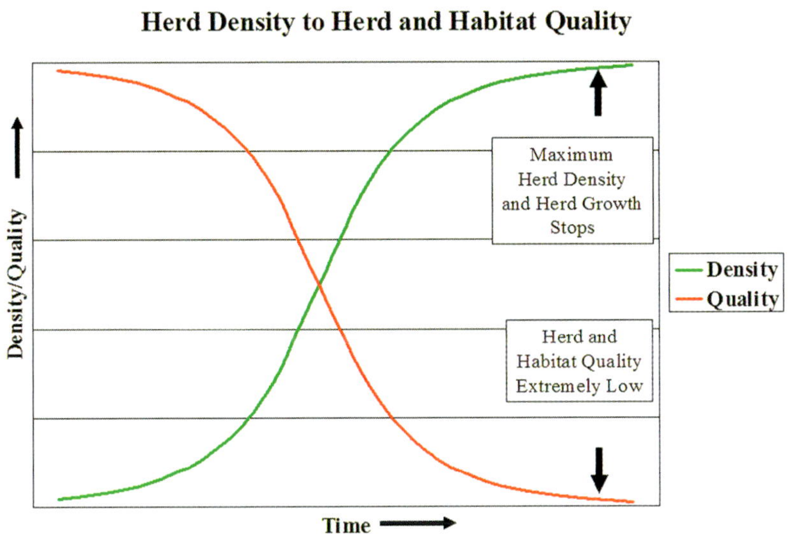

Figure 6-7. Farther to the right on the graph's timeline, the herd's growth rate slows dramatically. This is in direct response to the low quality of the habitat (red line). The burgeoning herd has consumed all of the top-quality food sources and, more than likely, most of the second-choice foods. At this point, the quality and health of individual deer are low.

Each doe's diet consists primarily of poor foods. Does can barely ingest enough food for their own survival, let alone produce the extra nutrition required to develop a fetus and nurse a fawn. Thus, fewer fawns survive to be recruited into the herd.

High herd density in conjunction with low food availability also increases natural mortality in deer. In fact, in high deer-density areas, malnutrition can be a major cause of death. In these areas most deer are not starving to death, but malnutrition weakens them and makes them susceptible to disease or predation. The actual cause of death masks the direct link to malnutrition as the primary cause of mortality. This mortality is considered "density-dependent mortality," because the death rate of deer increases with herd density.

A deer herd at the far right on the graph, like the one depicted in the last of the Herd Density to Herd and Habitat Quality graphs, will display declines in individual deer health. Everyone understands if an animal is not fed well, its body weight and performance will decline. But the relationship between food volume and quality and reproductive success is not as obvious. What is meant by "poor reproductive success?" Are the does not being bred? No. The answer is fawn mortality. Even in a seriously underfed deer herd, most does become pregnant. However, poor food resources limit fetal development. With humans, poor nutrition for an expectant mother can cause her child to have a low birth weight, which is linked to long-term poor health. The same is true of deer. Poor nutrition during pregnancy causes fawns to be born underweight. Not only is an underweight fawn more susceptible to disease, but it may be so weak it cannot stand to nurse and may survive only hours to a few days.

Other nutrition-related causes of fawn mortality include poor milk production in does. Nutritionally stressed females may not produce enough milk to feed their fawns, and the fawns soon die of starvation or malnutrition-related diseases.

In addition, nutritionally stressed females may not produce hormones that trigger the mothering instinct, causing the mother to reject her offspring. In highly stressed herds, new mother does often abandon their fawns.

In all of these examples, females are still breeding and even giving birth, but newborn fawn mortality is high. Hunters often assume their herd has no problem with fawn mortality because they don't see dead fawns in spring and summer. However, newborn fawns are small and have soft, uncalcified bones. Predators and scavengers eat the carcass, leaving no sign of the fawns' presence or death. Even in areas with extremely high fawn mortality rates, finding dead fawns is uncommon.

Carrying Capacity

Those familiar with herd-growth dynamics and habitat limitations will notice little reference to the term "carrying capacity" in this discussion. We have avoided using this phrase because it is vague. What exactly is it? A common definition for carrying capacity is "the maximum number of deer a particular habitat can support." The problem with this definition is

Changing food sources through the seasons and variations in rainfall can produce substantial swings in annual food production and quality.

defining the level of support. Support at a healthy level? Support at the starvation level? What stage of a herd's health is the cut-off point?

Unfortunately, a definitive point at which deer begin to starve cannot be established. In fact, density-dependent mortality far exceeds actual starvation in any habitat. As shown in the density/quality graph, declines in herd health are gradual. Even before adult deer begin starving to death, most fawns have died from malnutrition. No matter what level of "support" defines carrying capacity, a cut-off point is not obvious. For any habitat, there is no particular density at which deer health suddenly switches from good to bad. We should point out that habitat can be as dynamic as the deer herd, with food sources changing through the seasons, and with variations in rainfall and growing conditions producing substantial swings in food production and quality.

Over the past few generations, deer biologists, managers, and hunters have seen the full spectrum of density-quality relationships. Early management practices strived to increase deer numbers in areas with extremely low deer densities. However, the quality of these early-restoration herds was extremely high. We've all seen the old black-and-white photos of giant bucks harvested during the early days of deer restoration. Few deer were available for hunting, but those bagged were whoppers! These herds were at the far left of the density-quality graph.

Today, the opposite is true. Across the whitetail's range, deer are usually so abundant that managers strive to control or reduce herd numbers. In these high-density herds, deer quality is poor. Even fully mature deer are "stunted" by poor nutrition.

Photo by Jim Winch

When deer numbers were low during the restoration period, ample forage produced some truly impressive deer.

This is the common age class deer brought back to most camps in America.

Hunters often mistakenly blame this "stunting" on poor genetics. The real culprit is poor nutrition and overpopulation. These herds are near the far right of the density-quality graph.

To use another analogy, let's examine a hypothetical fishing pond. When a pond has enough forage for all of the bass to eat, they will continue to grow larger with age. The more forage that is available, the bigger and faster the bass grow. But as their numbers become more abundant than the available forage, bass stop growing larger. They may even decline in size as forage continues to diminish. Unless more forage is introduced and/or more fish are removed, these bass will remain stunted. Just because they get older does not mean they will get bigger.

The Density-Quality Relationship Through The Hunter's Eye

We presented the density/quality graph as an example of how a herd's growth rate changes over time, and how herd and habitat quality are inversely related to herd density. But we can look at it another way. Deer herds are managed through selective removal, or hunter harvest. Again, the trigger finger is the ultimate deer-management tool. By annually removing the same number of deer that are born and survive to adulthood, hunters can help hold a deer population at steady levels. In fact, this can be accomplished through a combination of hunter harvest and natural mortality. This combination of hunter harvest and natural mortality stops the herd's growth, or stops the progression of the graph further toward the right side. In essence, you can hold herd density-and the corresponding herd and habitat quality-at any desired point. The big question is "where" to aim on the density-quality graph.

Different groups of hunters will have different goals. Harvest rates should be calculated accordingly.

It should be noted that "holding a herd steady" is not a completely accurate term. Herd densities and habitat qualities are dynamic. They are not static or steady, but always changing. For example, an acorn crop might be large in an area one year, and then be a total failure the next. Although herds and habitat are dynamic, you can aim your management toward a general range of values on the graph.

Habitat Types

Numerous habitat types exist throughout the whitetail's range. The density/quality graph is based on an average or Standard Model habitat. No numbers appear on the vertical or horizontal scales of the hypothetical example because actual

A combination of mixed timber and agricultural fields can support an extremely healthy herd at 40-50 deer per square mile.

deer densities and the timeline depend on specific types of habitat.

For example, in a mature hardwoods environment, one that commonly produces low quantities of forage, the far right of the graph might occur when the population is around 15 to 20 deer per square mile. In this largely unproductive habitat, the inflection point would be eight to 10 deer per square mile. On the other hand, a habitat of 50 percent mixed timber and 50 percent agricultural crops may not reach the far right of the graph until the density reaches 80 to 100 or more deer per square mile, and the inflection point of maximum herd growth would occur at approximately 40 to 50 deer per square mile.

Whitetail herds in most habitat types follow the Standard Model, with deer density numbers and inflection

An expanse of mature forest provides limited deer habitat.

points varying by the exact make-up of the habitat (food production and quality). Yet, a few unique habitats produce different density/quality patterns.

Whitetail herds in most habitat types follow the Standard Model, with deer density numbers and inflection points varying by the exact make-up of the habitat.

Low Productivity Habitat

In what we refer to as a Low Productivity Habitat, the quantity of deer food is high, but the food's nutritional value is low. A good example is the Coastal Plain of the Southeastern U.S. A high volume of plants grows in these semi-tropical environments, but because of the poor-quality sandy soils, plants have low levels of nutrients.

From a management standpoint, herd densities in Low Productivity Habitat can be held at a variety of levels with few differences in herd/habitat quality. Herd health may be similar at densities of 10 deer per square mile or 50 deer per square mile. Ten deer per square mile may be well beyond the inflection point. But the high volume of poor-quality food might support 50 deer per square mile just as easily and with nearly equal levels of herd performance.

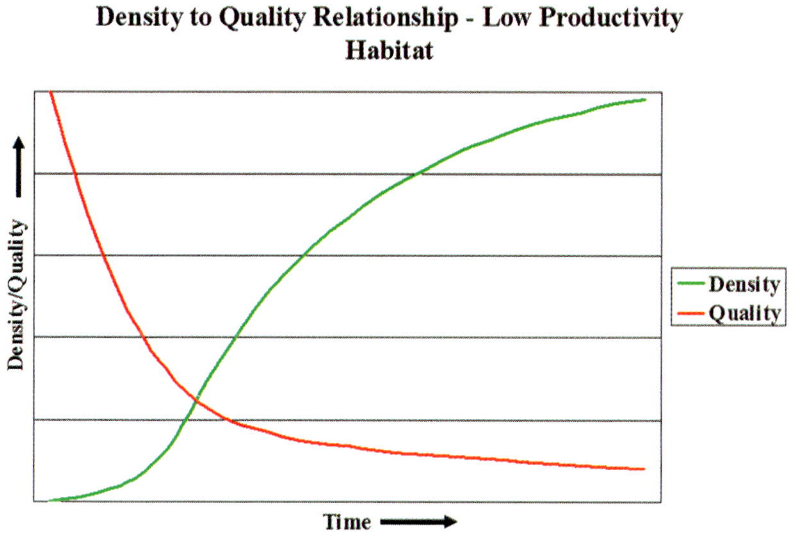

Figure 6-8. Because of poor-quality food sources in Low Productivity Habitat, the herd/habitat quality line on the graph declines much more rapidly than in a Standard Model Habitat. This also means the inflection point is much farther to the left on the graph. In this habitat, even a low density of deer can rapidly consume the limited, top-choice foods. The health of individual animals also declines rapidly at even minimal increases in herd densities. Yet, because of the high volume of food sources in a Low Productivity Habitat, herd growth and the potential for a maximum number of deer are not as closely tied to the habitat's quality. Even though herd and habitat quality rapidly bottom out on the graph, the herd continues to grow.

In a situation like this, hunters must harvest a high percentage of deer to show improvements in herd and habitat quality. In fact, to reduce a deer population to near or below the inflection point might be beyond the ability of most hunter/managers. Even if this low density could be accomplished, the low density would certainly produce deer sightings well below the level required for an enjoyable or acceptable hunt.

Many biologists believe Low Productivity Habitat deer herds are not density dependent. This thinking results from management projects that have reduced deer densities without a corresponding improvement in herd quality. We believe these herds are indeed density dependent, but the whitetail population must be reduced much more than in a Standard Model habitat to increase the quality of the deer. Most managers and researchers have failed, or aren't willing, to reduce deer numbers far enough or maintain them at low enough densities to increase the quality. In their defense, just as a threshold exists in the relationship between whitetails and their habitat, a threshold also exists for hunter satisfaction, which deer managers and biologists usually must maintain. For the most part, deer hunters pay their salaries, directly or indirectly. In Low Productivity Habitat, reducing herd densities far enough to produce a desired improvement in herd health would require deer densities be well below what most hunters would find acceptable. From an overall management standpoint, no one desires unhappy hunters.

From a management viewpoint, it is often easier to increase the quantity of quality food production by establishing food plots and improving native vegetation than to reduce the herd density enough to increase its quality. The plow and the ax are more important in this environment than the trigger finger for improving the herd, at least initially. However, once the herd responds to its improved food sources, the trigger finger must be used liberally to maintain the appropriate herd density for the habitat quality.

Photo by George Barnett

When deer sightings become few and far between, hunter satisfaction diminishes greatly.

When forage is limited, developing food plots and openings in the canopy can greatly increase the quantity and quality of the preferred habitat for deer on a specific property.

Agricultural Habitat

Large-scale Agricultural Habitat also does not fit the standard density-quality graph. This type of habitat exists across a wide swath of the whitetail's range, including the agricultural areas of the Midwest and Great Plains. Pockets of Agricultural Habitat also exist across the Southeastern U.S. and along the Atlantic Seaboard.

As compared to a Low Productivity Habitat, extensive croplands produce the opposite effects on whitetails. The nearly unlimited availability of top-choice food sources produces very high herd and habitat quality even when deer densities are high. This shifts the inflection point on the graph far to the right. The quantity and quality of food sources are so high in these areas that deer numbers often exceed "social carrying capacity" before the herd displays serious declines in health. Social carrying capacity is the maximum number of deer a human population will tolerate. Car-deer collisions, Lyme's disease, and other diseases linked to deer, crop depredation, and damage to homeowners' ornamental trees and shrubs all play roles in determining an area's social carrying capacity.

The dominance/subordination process appears to cause health-related problems when populations are unnaturally high. Individual deer performance (i.e., body weight, antler development and reproductive success) declines dramatically in a high-density herd, especially among deer low on the social ladder. Before they run out of high-quality foods, whitetails in an Agricultural Habitat often reach densities high enough to cause social-interaction problems. In this situation, herd density plays a greater role in determining herd quality than food resources.

The Relationship of Herd Density to Herd and Habitat Quality

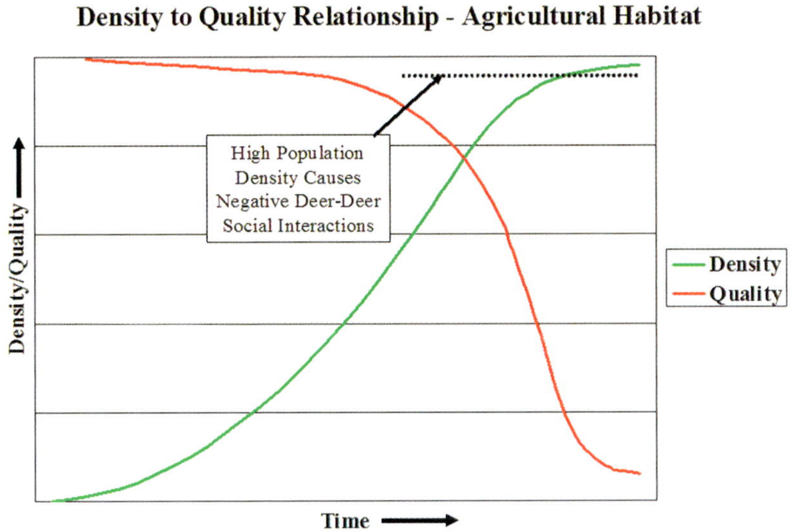

Figure 6-9. From a management perspective, such a high volume of good food is available in an Agricultural Habitat that the density of a deer herd has to be extraordinarily high before a decline in herd quality is seen. Usually, the herd far surpasses the social carrying capacity before it begins to show a decline in health because of poor nutrition.

Another factor in the density/quality relationship of deer in an Agricultural Habitat is social stress. Experiments have shown that a deer herd held at a very high density displays declines in health even when nutrition is excellent. In the above graph, notice the dotted line indicating the population density causing negative social interactions. These negative deer-deer social interactions cause herd health to decline and population growth to stagnate, long before the habitat's food resources are exhausted. In this situation, the negative social interactions among deer are the limiting factors to population growth, instead of food resources.

The nearly unlimited availability of top-choice food sources in vast agricultural areas produces very high herd and habitat quality even when deer densities are high.

Photo by George Barnett

In agricultural areas, the herd usually far surpasses the social carrying capacity before it begins to show a decline in health due to nutrition .

Improving Deer Herd Quality

To improve the quality of a deer herd on a property, the "herd density to herd and habitat quality" relationship cannot be overlooked. Hunters and deer managers often forget this essential point, but there is no way around this relationship. No shortcuts can fix density-quality problems with whitetails. In essence, if a herd is toward the right of the graph, then maximizing deer potential is impossible. This fact cannot be overstated. We consider the density-quality relationship to be another absolute law of wildlife management.

When the herd's density is toward the right of the graph, the herd quality can be improved in three ways. The quickest and least expensive road to improved herd health is to reduce deer numbers with increased use of the trigger finger. By increasing the harvest, the herd's density can be lowered and shifted toward the left on the graph, thereby increasing herd quality. Those who do not have total control of the habitat they hunt and manage-a lease situation, for example-this is the only viable option.

The second means of improving herd quality is to increase the amount of high-quality food produced by the habitat. This might entail thinning timber, planting food plots, doing controlled burns, and applying herbicides. This shifts herd density leftward on the graph by "raising the bar" of habitat quality. However, this process requires the hunter/manager control the habitat.

Lastly, and certainly the best way to improve the quality of whitetails on a property, is to do both-shoot more deer while increasing the habitat's productivity. Decreasing the number of deer decreases the competition for top-quality food sources-

Photo by George Barnett

Providing an environment with ample nutrition, cover, water, and limited social stress through habitat and trigger finger management is the key that will open the door to a successful deer management program.

enough to get ahead of the herd's browsing pressure. Once habitat improvements are established, they will remain most productive if browse pressure is kept low.

Assessing a Habitat

Assessing the position of a deer herd on the density/quality graph may be difficult for inexperienced hunters/managers. However, the best indicator of the density-quality relationship is the condition of the available forage in an area.

Overabundant herds - those far to the right on our graph-often cause "browse lines." The type of plants in an area, the severity of the browse lines, and the seasons of the year are important considerations when assessing herd density-habitat conditions. A severely overpopulated herd produces browse lines on low-choice food sources not only during a "seasonal stress period" when feed is most limited, but also at other times of the year. Browse lines are a warning signal. They tell you deer have limited food sources, and, consequently, cannot express their full potential.

When assessing a habitat, detailed knowledge of food sources is essential. Managers must know the food resources available, as well as their preference and nutritional value to deer. Although this information seems basic, it is often overlooked.

In any given region or habitat, weather patterns produce seasonal deficiencies in food production. For example, an oak forest might produce a huge volume of acorns in fall. In a bumper acorn year, so many acorns may be available that fall food sources are essentially unlimited. But during other seasons of the year, or in fall during a poor acorn year, deer forage might be scarce. During spring and summer, the forest's leafy canopy blocks out sunlight, greatly reducing the growth of plants within reach of deer. This lack of browse during summer certainly means very low food availability during winter, especially following a poor acorn crop.

To gain an accurate picture of browse pressure, habitat must be assessed when food sources are most limited. This is usually during the peak seasonal stress period, which determines the upper limits of a deer population in any area. In an oak forest, late-winter is the primary stress period for deer, because that is when food sources are most limited. In other regions, such as Texas, a hot, dry summer may be the primary stress time. Some Southern regions have two stress periods, both late winter and hot, dry periods in late summer.

Assessing a habitat at the wrong time of year, especially assessing browse pressure when the most food sources are available to deer, produces an inaccurate picture of the herd's relationship to the habitat. For example, in a hardwood habitat, monitoring browse pressure during spring green-up, or in a fall when acorns are abundant, gives a false impression of the habitat's condition. Those times are when food sources are the least limited. The appropriate time to assess habitat is the late-winter stress period. Similarly, assessing an arid deer habitat after a period of good rainfall also produces incorrect results. An arid habitat should be reviewed during the driest months, or during the seasonal stress period.

Another excellent method of assessing habitat quality, especially when monitoring trends over several years, is recording and analyzing physical condition data from harvested deer.

Herds that become overabundant often leave browse lines, such as the one above this ATV.

These data include age, body weights, lactation rates, and antler development from each deer harvested on the site. For example, comparing the body weights of 2½-year-old does from year to year provides an indication of the habitat quality each year.

Photo by George Barnett

Stress periods for whitetails are dependant on habitat, geographic location, and water conditions.

Photo by George Peacon

Another excellent method of assessing habitat quality, especially when monitoring trends over several years, is recording and analyzing physical condition data from harvested deer.

The Relationship of Herd Density to Herd and Habitat Quality

Browse assessment is an excellent tool for making a one-time evaluation of a property. This is useful when considering buying or leasing a new place to hunt. However, the use of physical condition indices, such as body weights, is an excellent method to track the herd/habitat quality relationship over time.

compensate for the lack of nutritious foods once available. Also, more deer/human interactions occur when deer seek new sources of food, such as in flower or vegetable gardens or in clover planted along roadways.

The habitat damage also affects birds, reptiles, and amphibians that share this area. Many bird species nest within five feet of the ground and, therefore, require thick brush to hide nests from predators. This also is the height a hungry deer can reach for feeding. In an overpopulated environment, deer eat all available nesting cover, causing low-nesting birds to disappear.

The low-growing plants deer eat also provide shady, moist conditions required by numerous species of reptiles and amphibians. The loss of these plants by deer overbrowsing

Deer begin to look for new sources of food, such as in flower or vegetable gardens, when natural vegetation becomes depleted.

damages this critical reptile and amphibian habitat and may cause serious declines in their populations.

Maximum Buck Harvest Management

Maximum Buck Harvest Management was designed to allow maximum harvest of bucks while allowing the deer population to expand rapidly. Maximum Buck Harvest Management (MBHM) is also called "traditional" or "restoration" management and is the original form of deer management most agencies followed while restoring deer herds. History has shown this management effectively increased deer populations throughout the whitetail's range.

Photo by Ole Torgersen

Hunters in "traditional hunting" zones are very familiar with this picture.

Photo by George Barnett

Under Maximum Buck Harvest Management, protecting does-the fawn producers-is the main goal.

Photo by George Barnett

In most cases, under Maximum Buck Harvest Management 80-90% of the annual buck harvest will be yearlings.

"Hands Off" and Maximum Buck Harvest Management

Studies show a small number of bucks can effectively breed a substantial number of does. Thus, protecting does is critical to sustaining high fawn production each year. Based on these studies, MBHM allows most bucks to be harvested while protecting does. Unfortunately, adult sex ratios become increasingly unbalanced over time as hunters harvest a large percentage of the adult male population each year, while not harvesting does. Under MBHM, protecting does-the fawn producers-is the main goal. Most hunters and managers believed that more does in an area produced more male fawns for future harvest.

During deer restoration, MBHM benefited hunters by allowing buck harvests while rapidly rebuilding the herds. Under MBHM, hunters could see many deer per hunting day and could harvest any buck. Some managers still believe the number of deer observed per day is the primary factor influencing hunter satisfaction. Although MBHM produces abundant deer for viewing, continuing this management over many years will not necessarily produce maximum buck harvests. Additionally, the quality of the average buck harvested under MBHM is low. Where MBHM has been practiced for many years, 70 percent or more of the annual buck harvest may be yearling (1½ years old) bucks.

Although deer have been restored to most, if not all, of their original range, some agencies continue to practice MBHM.

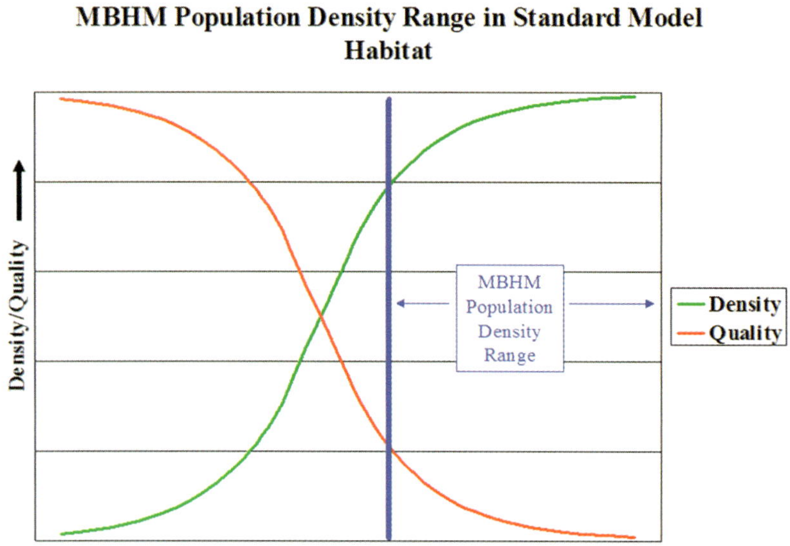

Figure 7-1. When examining the Density to Quality graphs in this and following chapters, no longer consider them "time-lines." These graphs still display the population growth curve, but remember that hunter harvest is used to reduce, stop or reverse the growth of a deer herd. By removing deer from the population, hunters alter the herd's growth rate. Depending on the number of deer harvested, the process of population growth can be slowed, halted or reversed.

Hunter harvest is not the only way to alter the position of herd density on the Density to Quality graph. Significantly improving the habitat will push the position of herd density down and to the left on the graph, producing results similar to decreasing the herd's density. However, without increased hunter harvest, this leftward shift on the graph would be only temporary, as the herd's improved reproductive success would cause herd density to rapidly increase back and to the right on the graph.

Cont. from page 124. Without hunter harvest, the natural process of herd growth will always move the population density rightward on the graph, toward the level where population size is maximized and herd growth stops. How many deer must be harvested to hold a population from growing larger depends on the current density of the herd and its position on the Density to Quality Graph. If herd growth without hunter harvest would be slow, such as at the far left or far right of the graph, few deer need to be harvested to keep the population from growing. If herd density is in a rapid growth section of the curve, such as at the inflection point, then many more deer need to be harvested annually to hold the population stable.

In the Figure 7-1, herd density in an MBHM herd is very high while herd quality, including reproductive success, is very low. Few deer will be annually recruited into this type of herd, hence hunter harvest need not be high to keep the herd from further growth.

The Biology of MBHM

A long-term MBHM program produces few, if any, advantages to a herd. Once a deer herd is restored, MBHM keeps the deer herd at a high density in relation to habitat conditions. (The actual deer densities in an MBHM program vary by habitat type.) When considering the Herd Density to Herd and Habitat Quality graph, MBHM keeps the deer herd at the far right of the graph. Overall herd density is high, but herd and habitat quality are low.

In Low Productivity habitat, the inflection point on the Herd Density to Herd and Habitat Quality graph is so low most herds fall into the MBHM density range. Rarely do herd managers reduce deer populations in these areas to the inflection

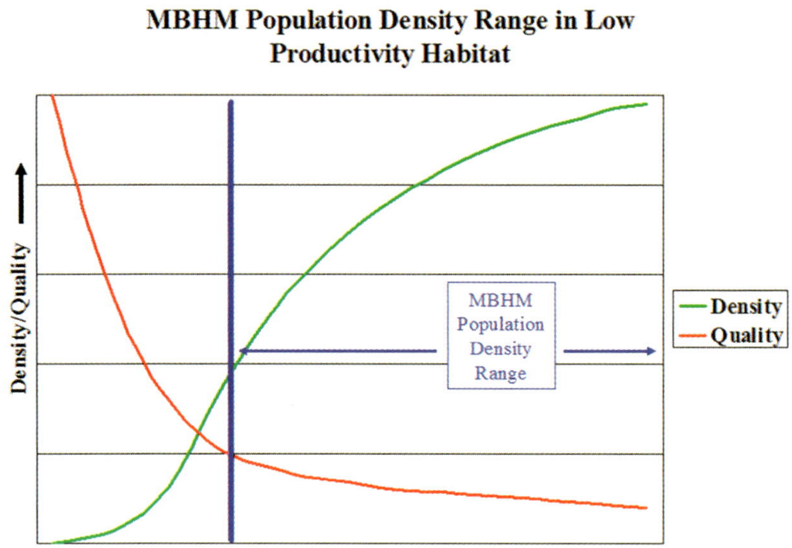

Figure 7-2. In Low Productivity habitat, the limiting factor for herd productivity and health is not the amount of food, but the quality of the food. In this habitat condition, a herd at 20 deer per square mile may produce herd health similar to a herd at 50 deer per square mile. Because such a broad area of the graph fits into an MBHM-herd model, tight maintenance of herd densities is not as critical as in other habitat types. Changes in deer density-even substantial changes-may exhibit little, if any, change in herd or habitat quality.

point. The low inflection point for these herds also produces a wide range of density numbers that stay within the MBHM portion of the curve.

In Standard Model habitat, an MBHM herd can have a wide range of deer density figures, but these density numbers are specific to each habitat. Unlike Low Productivity habitats, where a wide range of deer densities produce similarly low herd and habitat quality, each standard habitat has a fairly distinct range of densities that fall into the MBHM range. The variations arise because of differences in habitat food production, especially during stress periods (winter and/or late summer). For example, a mature forest habitat produces little winter forage for deer. In these areas, an MBHM herd may be as low as 15 to 20 deer per square mile. On the other hand, a mixed habitat of varying-age forests and 20 to 30 percent agriculture could yield a much higher density because more winter food is available. In this habitat, an MBHM herd may exceed 60 deer per square mile and still produce the same herd/habitat quality conditions as the 15 deer per-square-mile herd in mature hard woods. The mixed habitat produces more food during stress periods, thus maintaining a higher deer density.

Photo by George Barnett

A mature hardwood or pine forest habitat produces very little winter forage for deer.

Controlling deer densities in Standard Model habitat is important. Unlike Low Productivity areas, Standard Model habitat can be severely damaged by deer densities that are too high. Herd health can also suffer dramatically from overpopulation.

MBHM herds in Agricultural habitat are controlled by several factors other than food availability. In Agricultural habitat, deer enter the stress period (winter) in great condition and can maintain body weights at acceptable levels until spring green-up. In intensive Agricultural habitat, little natural habitat remains, and is usually limited to creek drainages and land not suited for tillage. In these areas deer usually consume all plants except mature trees and undesirable species. The herds primarily eat agricultural crops during the growing season and unharvested crops during winter. In these areas, herd density is limited by "social" carrying capacity and herd dynamics. The "social carrying capacity" is the maximum number of deer the human population will tolerate. At some point, crop depredation and car-deer collisions become intolerable to residents. In Agricultural habitat, this peak deer density is reached well before it is high enough to consume the amount of quality forage produced by agricultural crops.

Whether it is practiced in a Low Productivity, Standard, or Agricultural model habitat, MBHM produces large deer numbers. These deer are often very observable, not only because of the high density, but also because they must travel farther to find food. Many agencies believe numerous deer sightings are a prime factor in hunter satisfaction. Although MBHM produces high deer sightings, most are of does and poor-quality yearling bucks.

MBHM Population Density Range in Agricultural Habitat

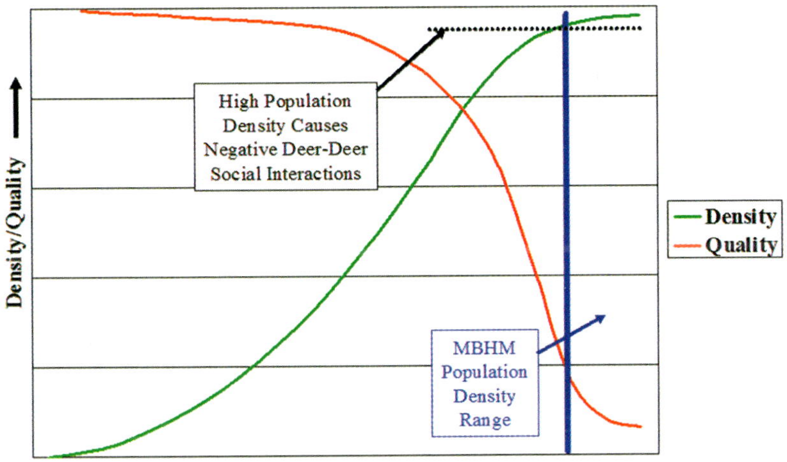

Figure 7-3. In Agricultural habitat, the primary limiting factor to herd growth is herd social dynamics. Very high deer densities can impair individual deer health, performance, and reproductive success because of social conflicts arising from large numbers of deer living too close to each other. Just as stress can produce a variety of diseases and health problems in humans, conflicts over dominance and even "space" can produce serious stress-related health problems in deer. These declines occur well before food resources become limited. Research at the Cusino Research facility in Michigan found that herd health declined rapidly at densities above 100 deer per square mile, simply because of negative social interactions, even though ample food resources were available. In fact, in Agricultural habitat, MBHM population densities are usually near or above the density required to cause negative deer social interactions.

Photo by George Barnett

Herd health can decline due to social stress, even though ample food sources are available.

Because MBHM densities are held at the far right of the Herd Density to Herd-Habitat Quality graph, habitat conditions and individual deer health are generally poor. Too many mouths are competing for limited food resources. Not only is food quantity a problem in these situations, but top-quality food sources are often browsed beyond their ability to regrow each year, and eventually disappear. In MBHM areas, first-choice (highly nutritious) deer food often can't regrow - and it may be common to see browse lines on poor food sources as deer are forced to subsist on low-nutrition plants. Because most foods are of low nutrition and digestibility, deer cannot express their genetic potential, even at maturity.

Although MBHM allows a high buck harvest, heavy harvest pressure on bucks without an equal harvest of does skews the adult sex ratio heavily toward females. In addition,

Since the majority of food intake in overpopulated areas involves plants of low nutritional quality, individual deer cannot express their full genetic potential, even at maturity. This browse line speaks volumes for this particular property.

Photo by George Barnett

As deer populations continue to rise, the remedy is to shoot more does.

most bucks are yearlings, because harvest removes most bucks long before they reach maturity. The skewed sex ratio and young buck age structure causes many negative social and biological complications within the herd. When adult sex ratios and age structures are skewed from the way they were before the Europeans settled the United States, it stands to reason that herd health and performance will decline.

Unfortunately, many agencies failed to inform the hunting public that once deer herds were fully restored, they would need to switch to different management. This new management-a "sustained yield" management-would be driven by a need to hold the deer density stable. The problem is that sustained yield management requires a substantial doe harvest. Hunters, having been exposed to restoration management for most, if not all, of their hunting careers, incorporated the "never shoot a doe" philosophy into their hunting ethics. In areas that have been under an MBHM program for generations, it can be difficult to convince hunters that harvesting does is necessary and biologically sound. Consequently, the transition to sustained yield management can be complex. But without question, this transition can be and is successfully implemented when hunters work toward that goal.

Some agencies have failed to switch management styles. Even after restoration is complete, whether because of "tradition," financial, or other factors, these agencies do not shift their MBHM to sustained-herd oriented practices. In many situations, agencies are not completely to blame. Political pressure placed on agencies by the hunting public prevents agencies from adopting adequate doe harvest guidelines. Needless to say, this leads to further herd growth and eventually to overpopulation and habitat depletion.

In most MBHM-managed herds, overall health is poor, the herd's social structure is unnatural, and the habitat remains poor from years of overbrowsing. Because MBHM has been practiced for many years in most areas of the country, deer hunters and managers now face the problems associated with MBHM.

The MBHM Hunting Experience

Most hunters are familiar with the experience of hunting a MBHM deer herd. One of the most recognizable advantages to hunting MBHM herds is that hunting over food sources can be very productive. Because food sources are limited, deer must travel farther for food and are forced to feed for longer periods. In a MBHM herd, it is common to see large groups of deer feeding in agricultural fields and food plots. However, most of them are antlerless. Hunters in these situations often report 30 or more antlerless deer per antlered buck, although these observed sex ratios do not accurately represent the actual adult sex ratio. Many of the observed "does" are actually button bucks, or yearling bucks born so late their antlers aren't visible. However, these highly skewed antlerless-to-antlered ratios are accurate "perceptions" of the sex ratio and are part of the MBHM hunting experience. More antlered bucks may actually be in the herd, but because of skewed sex ratios and heavy harvest pressure, bucks rarely show themselves during daylight, especially in fields, because doing so could prove fatal.

Another popular aspect of the MBHM hunting experience is liberal buck harvests. Bound only by agency-imposed bag limits, bucks can be harvested at will without a minimum standard. Although it was originally thought MBHM would produce the maximum number of bucks for harvest, more recent research suggests this may not be the case.

The downside of hunting a MBHM herd is that few large bucks are seen. As many hunters suspect, the low number of buck sightings is caused in part by heavy harvest pressure, forcing bucks into nocturnal movement-especially the few older, more experienced bucks. However, the lack of older-age buck sightings is not only because of nocturnal movement. Many hunters reassure themselves a bunch of old mossy-horned bucks are out there, but are just totally nocturnal. In reality, older bucks may not exist. In MBHM herds, so many bucks are harvested as yearlings (sometimes 80 to 90 percent of the entire yearling buck population), that few survive to their second year of adulthood, and almost no bucks reach maturity.

The poor adult sex ratio and young buck age structure of an MBHM herd suppresses breeding competition. With many does and few bucks, little competition exists among bucks, and subsequently, there is little rutting activity and little sign-making, such as rubs and scrapes. Yearling bucks are not sexually mature enough to perform the full sequence of these rut markings. Those who have hunted their entire lives in MBHM herds often complain they see few rubs, no signpost rubs, and rarely see a scrape. While presenting our rub research to hunting groups in MBHM states, we have discovered most hunters in the group have never seen a true signpost rub.

The lack of competition among bucks in an MBHM herd has additional consequences for hunters. Without competition for breeding rights, bucks don't have to chase does, reducing their exposure during daylight when predator densities are high (legal hunting hours). They can wait until after dark and still have access to estrous does.

Few bucks in a population cause the breeding season to become extended, often lasting for months. Hunters call this a "trickle" rut, where short surges of rutting activity are observed, followed by long lulls. In these situations, it is common to hear hunters say the rut has "turned off," or is "on again." Although it appears the rut is turning "on and off," breeding activity remains constant. The few bucks in the herd need several months to work their way through the large doe population, and most of this occurs at night because there is no competition to drive it into daylight hours. The rut's "on" cycle can be attributed to peaks in daylight rutting activity caused by sudden turns in the weather that allow hunters to witness scattered rutting activity during daylight. Once the weather returns to more

The few bucks like this that happen to survive in a Maximum Buck Harvest Management program usually become nocturnal.

normal patterns, breeding activity returns primarily to nocturnal events.

The quality of the bucks in an MDHM herd is also compromised. Rut stress on individual bucks in such herds can have tragic results. The stress of a prolonged breeding season on a young buck already nutritionally stressed can cause lifelong reductions in body weight and can even cause stress-related death.

Body and antler development are driven primarily by age. Older bucks have larger antlers and bodies than younger bucks. Secondarily, nutrition is a major influence. In an MBHM herd, most observable bucks are young and, consequently, small. Nutritional resources in the high-density MBHM herds are limited, preventing deer of every age-class from reaching their full potential. Ultimately, MBHM herds are characterized by young buck populations that cannot reach their growth potential because of their youth and inadequate nutrition.

In addition to young age and poor nutrition, the strung-out breeding seasons of herds with poor sex-ratios cause some fawns to be born late in the summer. Does bred late in the breeding season give birth to fawns late in the fawning season. Fawns born late don't have as many months of growing time before the winter stress period arrives, resulting in poor growth as a fawn and stymied growth as a yearling. By the time late-born fawns reach their second November, they are only 15 or 16 months old, compared to the early-born fawns that are 18 or 19 months old. This two- to three-month age difference has a significant impact on antler development. Late-born buck fawns

Hunter conversations rarely include exciting tales about daylight rutting activity in Maximum Buck Harvest Management camps.

rarely produce more than spike antlers as yearlings. Note these spikes are not a result of "bad" genetics. They were simply born too late during the growing season to obtain enough nutrition to express their antler growth potential.

Because of limited food resources, skewed sex ratios, young buck age structure, strung-out breeding and fawning periods, and high rut stress on young bucks, the bucks harvested from MBHM herds are usually small in body and antler size.

Is MBHM Right for You?

After considering the experiences common to hunting in an MBHM herd, we must ask if these conditions meet hunters' desires. Historically, MBHM was used because it was thought to produce the highest harvest rates and, subsequently, highest hunter satisfaction ratings. Yet, numerous surveys show hunter satisfaction is not based on harvesting a deer, but rather on the quality of the experience.

In most hunter satisfaction surveys, hunters list "a safe hunting experience" as the most important factor. Also high on the list is knowing a mature buck exists in the hunting area and having a reasonable chance to harvest a mature, or "trophy" buck. In an MBHM herd, hunters see many antlerless deer, but have only a small chance of seeing, much less harvesting, mature bucks. In reality, there is a good chance trophy bucks do not exist in an MBHM herd.

MBHM Implementation and Maintenance

An MBHM program may seem easy to implement, and some aspects of this management are easy to apply. Different from the original forms of MBHM, harvest guidelines may include taking any antlered buck. However they must include an adequate doe harvest to hold the population stable.

As simple as it may seem, an MBHM herd can be difficult to maintain. It is much more challenging than most hunters/managers suspect to hold a high-density herd just below the maximum number of deer the habitat can support. A few too many deer and the habitat can be severely damaged, reducing the habitat's ability to feed deer-possibly permanently. A close watch is required to ensure the herd is not overbrowsing the habitat. This can be difficult, because detailed knowledge of food sources and plant-growth rates are required.

The total herd density, which is primarily controlled by doe harvests, must be held just below the food-production capacity of the habitat, which changes year to year and season to season. As discussed in Chapter 6, in an MDHM program, habitat assessments must be conducted annually. Because the herd density is already high, a sudden decrease in food sources could have drastic effects on herd health and future habitat production. One year of intense overbrowsing may limit a habitat's ability to produce deer foods for years. The sustained high deer density simply would not allow the habitat to "recover" from heavy overbrowsing, and many plants may have been browsed beyond their ability to regrow. Careful assessment of the habitat during the annual stress periods is necessary to ensure overbrowsing does not damage the habitat. Any sudden decline in food sources would need to be countered by an increased deer harvest, lowering the deer density below the level required to cause permanent habitat damage.

As we pointed out, deer herds and habitat quality are dynamic. That is, they are constantly changing. Production of

Photo by George Barnett

In all deer management programs, the hunter is the ultimate manager.

digestible and nutritious food sources are a prime example. A complete acorn crop failure in a primarily hardwood environment has drastic consequences on a deer herd that requires this high-fat food source to survive winter. A growing season drought would also drastically reduce winter foods deer rely on for survival. Even minor changes in habitat, such as an active agricultural field suddenly left to go fallow, may require corrective herd density measures, especially when that herd is already near maximum levels. Although the vital rules for a MDHM herd are fairly basic, keeping a high deer density within the habitat's ability to support it often requires considerable micro-management.

Photo by George Barnett

Chapter 8

Quality Deer Management

Quality Deer Management (QDM) is a strategy that includes harvest guidelines designed to establish and maintain herd characteristics similar to those present before Columbus landed in North America. These characteristics include a balanced adult sex ratio, older-age bucks (balanced age structure), and a density in balance with the habitat. A balanced adult sex

Photo by George Barnett

Just as the name implies, QDM provides for a quality hunting experience while at the same time managing for a quality deer herd.

ratio allows deer to express their physical potential, and also permits the herd to express a wider range of social activities, such as dominance-establishment and a full range of signpost communication. Because deer in a QDM herd follow more predictable seasonal patterns, we consider such herds more fun to hunt than MBHM herds.

As the name implies, QDM-Quality Deer Management-provides a quality hunting experience while managing for a quality deer herd. In other words, the goal is a combination of herd and habitat health, as well as hunter satisfaction.

The Biology Behind QDM

On the Herd Density to Herd-Habitat Quality for Standard Model graph, a QDM herd is held from just above the inflection point to approximately 80 percent of maximum.

Photo by Mick Hellickson

Hunters in a Quality Deer Management Program, as well as other deer management programs, are the ultimate deer managers.

Management programs do not have an exact cut-off point in herd density because environmental and habitat variations always come into play. Therefore, no exact numbers fit into

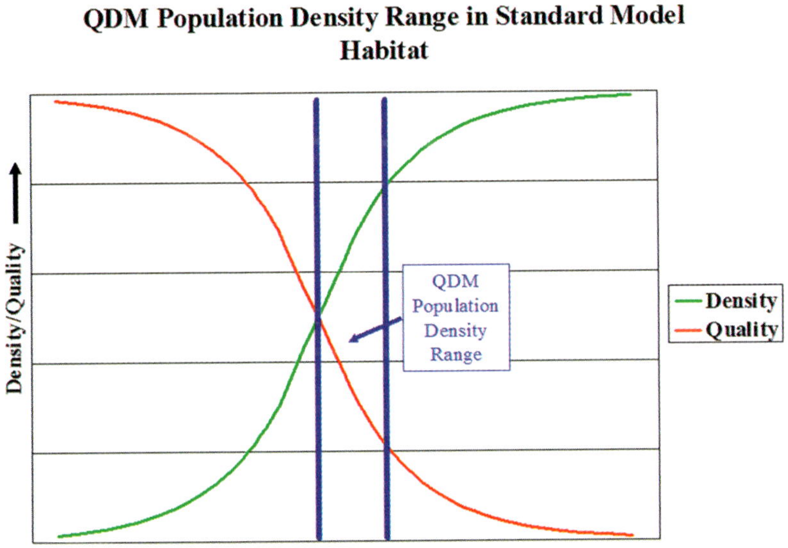

Figure 8-1. QDM really shines in Standard Model habitat. In these habitat situations, small changes in herd density often produce substantial changes in herd/habitat quality. More importantly, these changes can occur rapidly enough that hunters/managers easily see results in just a few years.

The population density range for QDM on the Standard Model Density to Quality Graph appears small compared to the range for MBHM. However, this is simply because the graph is a time-line type graph. If population densities appropriate for each management practice were displayed in another format, such as in the following example, the true differences become apparent.

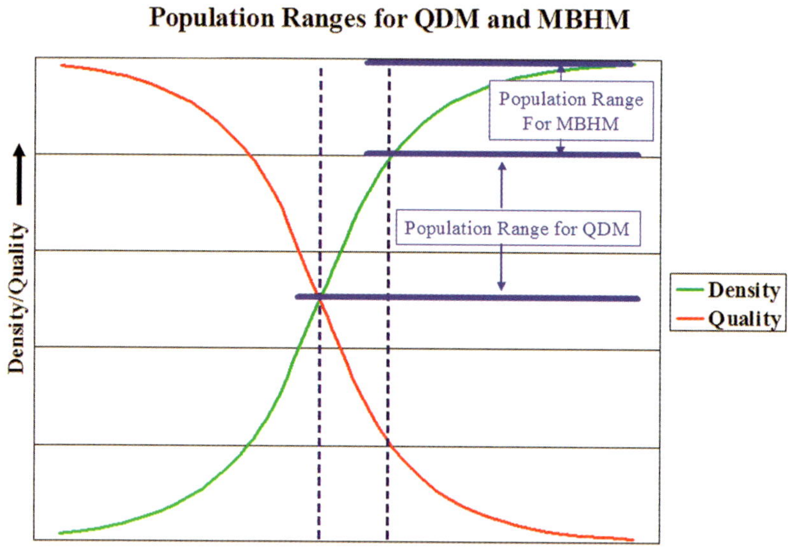

Figure 8-2. When the population ranges are illustrated vertically instead of horizontally along the growth curve, the larger range of actual population density numbers appropriate for QDM compared to MBHM become clearer. An unhunted deer herd in an area with no habitat improvement would rapidly grow through the QDM density range. Hunter harvest and/or habitat improvement are used to halt this rapid growth, holding the population within the fairly wide range of population densities displayed in the above example.

each management style, but a range of numbers overlap between management programs. Each deer-management program has a different philosophy for achieving specific goals, and each program strives to produce specific herd dynamics through a selective harvest strategy. In all of these management choices, hunters are the ultimate deer managers.

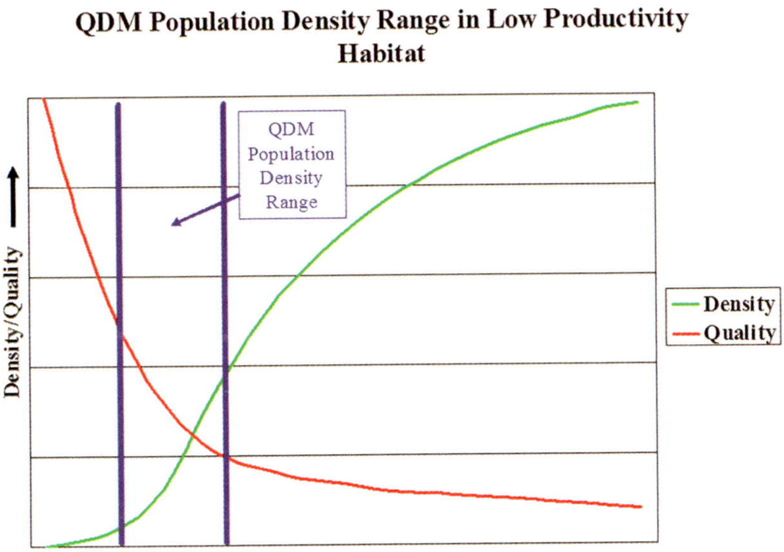

Figure 8-3. Keeping a Low Productivity Habitat herd in the QDM "zone" requires effort. Low Productivity habitat can support a broad zone of deer densities that coincide with MBHM, but very low herd densities are required to match herd parameters that are the cornerstone of QDM. Shifting herd density far enough leftward on the graph to match the QDM density-quality graph through hunter harvest alone (herd density reduction) may not be possible without improving the habitat. Additionally, the herd density required to match the QDM range through herd-density reduction may be too low to meet hunter desires. Hunter satisfaction is always a critical aspect of every management program.

A density below the inflection point certainly would mean a healthy herd and habitat, but would most likely fail to satisfy hunters. When the density is so low that deer sightings are few, hunter participation and recruitment are jeopardized. A herd above 80 percent of maximum-into the MBHM range-would produce many deer sightings, but herd performance

Photo by George Barnett

The Herd Density to Herd and Habitat Quality inflection point is so high that most agricultural habitat herds are already in the QDM zone.

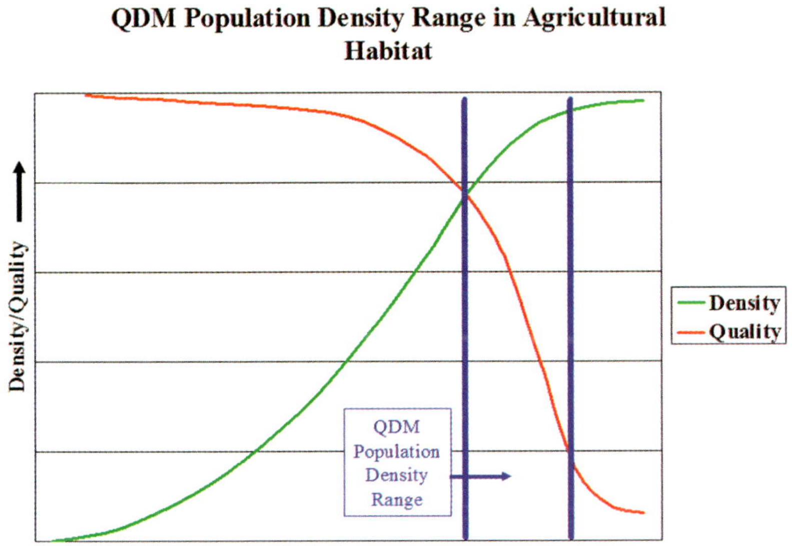

Figure 8-4. In Agricultural habitat, finding the right herd density for a QDM program is much easier than in Low Productivity or Standard Model habitat. The Herd Density to Herd and Habitat Quality inflection point is so high that most agricultural habitat herds are already in the QDM zone. The density required to leave the QDM range and enter the MBHM region far surpasses social carrying capacity. Because food resources are not as critical in agricultural regions, the primary concerns are human-deer interactions (social carrying capacity) and deer social interactions (herd dynamics). However, when crops have been harvested and food and cover become more of a limiting factor, the herd must be kept below the point at which they cause too many problems for the human population and below the point that negative herd social interactions occur.

Photo by George Barnett

Most Quality Deer Management programs strive for a deer density low enough for individual animal health and performance to be fairly high, while also providing enough deer sightings and harvest opportunities to satisfy hunters.

could suffer. Most QDM programs strive for a density just above the inflection point. This density is low enough for individual animal health and performance to be fairly high, while providing enough sightings and harvest opportunities to satisfy hunters.

The density required to meet QDM goals depends on habitat type and the amount and quality of stress-period food sources. In a predominantly mature forest habitat, with no access to agricultural crops, a QDM herd density of 10 to 12 deer per square mile may be appropriate. In a mixed agriculture and hardwood habitat, a density of 40 to 60 deer per square mile may still be in the QDM zone. In both cases, the limiting factor is quality food sources available during the seasonal stress periods.

QDM offers many biological advantages. Remember that QDM is designed to produce herds similar to the structure present before "the white man" managed this resource. A deer herd "functioning as intended" is a concept developed by studying deer herds managed by predators (Native Americans were possibly the most numerous white-tailed deer predators), and natural forces (wildfire, hurricanes, tornadoes, insect infestations in forests, etc.).

A QDM herd has an adult sex ratio no worse than one adult male for every two adult females. While a 1-1 ratio seems to maximize overall herd health, it is often difficult to achieve. With a ratio of one adult male to two adult females, the adult sex ratio will be balanced enough to produce herd dynamics that reflect pre-Columbus conditions. A balanced adult sex ratio encourages high competition among bucks that keeps the rut short, thus reducing overall rut stress in bucks.

The age structure of a QDM herd also has biological advantages. We suggest a QDM herd should have 30 percent of the bucks in the 3½-year-old or older category. The presence of older-age bucks is important to the herd's social dynamics. With enough mature bucks present, the rut begins earlier ensuring fawns have maximum growing time before winter. Quality male and female fawns are the cornerstone for future quality adult bucks and does. A herd and habitat relationship within the QDM range offers ample nutrition for fetal development and milk production, all of which increase fawn survival and growth.

With older bucks in the population, the processes of dominance and subordination work properly, reducing breeding activity and rut stress on younger bucks. Reduced breeding

Photo by George Barnett

When adult sex ratios are close to 1:1, the rut is both short and intense.

activity by younger bucks allows them to grow larger instead of expending bodily resources during their first rutting season. It allows them to become the dominant bucks of the future. Natural selection also occurs, with the largest, most aggressive bucks passing on their genetics at a higher rate.

A deer herd in the QDM density range also benefits from fewer social problems. A lower density herd is not forced into unnaturally close association. Just as long-term stress causes many health problems in humans, constant social battles between deer in high-density populations weaken herd performance. Experiments with deer held at very high densities found that deer suffer from many health and developmental problems. Even when given unlimited quantities of highly nutritious food,

Photo by George Barnett

Nutrition is a critical factor in fetal development, milk production, and fawn body growth, all of which increase fawn survival and growth.

Quality Deer Management is a compromise between hunter desires and herd dynamics.

high-density herds experience low fawn survival, stunted body growth, and under-developed antlers.

Few biological disadvantages are associated with QDM programs. Perhaps the closest thing to a problem in a well-managed QDM herd is that it's not in a totally natural state. QDM practices remain a compromise between "natural" conditions and hunter satisfaction. In a completely natural herd, the sex ratio would be nearly one-to-one, and a higher percentage of bucks would be in the fully mature age-classes (5½ years old or older). As is true of all forms of management, QDM tries to balance hunter desires and herd dynamics.

The QDM Hunting Experience

QDM is rapidly becoming the most popular form of management practiced by hunters. It has been implemented in many regions, with positive results. QDM has been practiced long enough that solid long-term scientific data are available documenting its benefits. Many articles, TV shows, and books describe how QDM produces high hunter satisfaction levels. These positive experiences are in areas where hunters are involved in the management process on their property. These are not claims from hunters paying large sums of money to hunt areas with quality or trophy deer. Much of the QDM practitioners' satisfaction results from interacting with a QDM herd and

Because most hunters practicing Quality Deer Management are directly involved with the success of their program, they have a greater sense of pride and ownership from the fruits of their labor.

the management process itself. Developing and succeeding in a QDM program produces a sense of stewardship, accomplishment, and extreme satisfaction among participating hunters.

Deer sightings are not as frequent in QDM herds compared to MBHM herds, but deer seen while hunting a QDM herd seem to provide more hunter satisfaction. Because a QDM herd has a more balanced adult sex ratio, buck sightings are more numerous in QDM herds than in MBHM herds. The balanced adult sex ratio influences deer to act differently than they do in an MBHM herd. Breeding competition creates more rutting sign such as rubs and scrapes. Our research indicates the number and size of rubs is closely linked to the number of bucks

Calling techniques, rattling, and decoys can be effective in a Quality Deer Management herd.

Photo by George Barnett

QDM herds will produce far more rubs per acre than an MBHM herd, and the average size of the rubs will be larger.

in the population, adult sex ratio, and most importantly, the percentage of bucks in the older age-classes. Bucks in QDM herds produce far more rubs than MBHM herds, and the average size of rubs will be larger. The older-age bucks of a QDM herd also produce signpost rubs. When considering hunter satisfaction, few things are more exciting than a site covered in huge rubs.

From the hunter's perspective, a successful QDM program provides additional benefits. Breeding competition encourages bucks to move more during daylight, especially during the rut. In a balanced herd with older-age bucks, the rut will be short, and breeding activity can reach an amazing frenzy. Buck sightings during the peak of the rut may be even higher than their actual representation in the herd. Bucks may move almost constantly during daylight in an attempt to breed as much as possible during the short-lived rut. This breeding frenzy also produces more daylight buck-doe chases, and it is not uncommon to see more than one buck chasing a "hot" doe.

Daylight buck activity is more predictable in a QDM herd, partly because competition forces bucks to move during daylight, but also because competition causes bucks to make more sign. Patterning mature bucks is easier when they are making rub and scrape lines. In addition, techniques such as calling, rattling, and decoying produce more responses if the sex ratio is balanced and older bucks are present. The presence of older bucks meets one of the most common factors in hunter satisfaction-the realistic opportunity to harvest a big buck.

Ironically, QDM requires high annual deer harvests, even though intuition suggests MBHM should produce the highest tolls. If more deer are roaming your property, then more deer should be available for harvest. However, to hold a

Quality Deer Management hunters will see more bucks and subsequently have to pass up more bucks to move them into the older age classes.

density stable over time, an equal number of animals must be removed as will be recruited into the herd through reproduction. Deer herds with densities near the inflection point produce the most surviving fawns. Therefore, holding these herds at that density level requires the maximum deer harvest rate possible for that herd. Requiring a high deer harvest is one problem most hunters don't mind.

From a hunter's standpoint, QDM has some downsides. The lower densities of QDM herds produce fewer sightings than herds under MBHM. In a QDM herd, hunters will not see 30 to 50 deer at a time feeding in agricultural fields and food plots. The higher doe harvests QDM requires make does increasingly wary. Doe social groups avoid feeding in fields during daylight. This is normal, but it's something most hunters hunting MBHM herds are not used to seeing.

Although hunters using QDM strategies usually see more bucks than those practicing MBHM, they must pass up young bucks. Some hunters new to QDM may find this difficult, but these young bucks must be allowed to grow into older bucks. Passing on them is critical.

Depending on the location, hunters may be required to harvest substantial numbers of does, especially during the early phases of a QDM program. When implementing a QDM program in an area previously managed under MBHM, harvesting enough does is difficult, not only because of the amount of hunting and harvesting required, but because many hunters are reluctant to harvest antlerless deer. Old traditions die hard, but hunters/managers must overcome this resistance to implement a successful QDM program.

In some habitat types, especially mixed agriculture/hardwoods, hunters may struggle to keep the deer herd in the QDM density zone. The high reproductive success produces more surviving fawns each year than hunters can remove from the adult deer population. As a result, herd density creeps back toward the right on the density-quality graph. Hunters/managers are often amazed by the high annual harvests required to hold QDM herds stable. We've frequently heard hunting clubs say, "This is going to sound crazy, but the more deer we shoot, the more deer we have." We reply, "You are exactly right. That is how deer dynamics work in productive habitat."

QDM Implementation and Maintenance

When designing a QDM program, the most important step is developing realistic goals that satisfy hunters and remain within the realm of possibility for the property in question. Many factors are important to consider: What are the habitat conditions? What is the herd density (where is the deer herd on the density-quality graph)? What is the buck age structure and adult sex ratio? Considering the size and shape of the area, how much influence will neighboring hunters have on management practices? How many are hunting the area? How long are the hunting seasons? How liberal are the bag limits? These factors affect which results can be achieved.

Hunters must first look at their land base, neighboring properties, local food sources, and other variables, and then set their goals accordingly.

When hunters are directly involved in the deer management on their property, success brings greater rewards than just a mount on the wall or venison in the freezer.

The goal that is most difficult to set, and achieve, is the standard for harvestable bucks. Many factors contribute to this decision, including the quality of bucks by age-class, the hunters' desires, the size of the property, the planned hunter density, and the habitat's quality. In essence, it is impossible to constantly produce several fully mature bucks with large antlers on an overpopulated, overbrowsed, small property with many hunters hunting long seasons.

Once a realistic buck age/size goal is determined, criteria must be established to prevent the harvest of bucks below the desired age/size. Typically it is necessary to limit the number of bucks each hunter can harvest or limit the size (age) of bucks that can be harvested. Different criteria can be used to limit the size/age of bucks eligible for harvest. Antler characteristics, such as spread and/or beam length, often work well, and in Low Productivity habitat, antler points can be used. As hunters become more experienced at field-judging bucks, body conformation is probably the best criterion for assessing age.

Even if most hunters on a given property decide to participate in QDM, a few individuals usually oppose any change. Use data from similar programs to support your harvest and habitat management plans to educate the naysayers. How you deal with those who disregard the QDM harvest regimen is up to you and the other hunters on your property.

Tracking the herd's progress is vital and requires good record keeping. A standardized system of data collection must be established to track deer observation rates and calculate sex ratios and reproductive success. Harvest data (body weight, age, sex, lactation in adult females, etc.) needs to be collected for tracking herd health.

Everyone involved with the program must learn more about deer biology, deer identification, and habitat conditions. Without question, education is a primary key to a successful program. Investing time and energy into the program automatically increases knowledge of the animal and its habits. Most hunters ultimately believe that participating in such a program increases their hunting skills and their hunting satisfaction.

Photo by George Barnett

Chapter 9

Trophy Deer Management

Although Trophy Deer Management (TDM) programs attract much attention, a truly successful TDM program is beyond the means of most deer hunters and managers. With that said, we don't mean to discourage those interested in a TDM program. It is important to understand that a successful TDM program is costly, including land, time, and money. Hunting such areas can cost upward of $10,000 per hunt, which sheds light on what it would cost to implement TDM on your

Photo by George Barnett

Successful Trophy Deer Management programs can and do exist throughout the whitetail's range.

TDM Population Density Range in Low Productivity Habitat

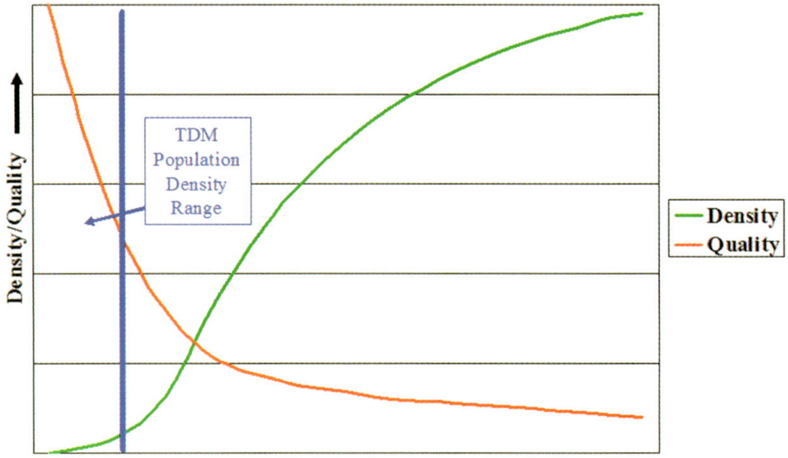

Figure 9-2. In Low Productivity habitat, TDM is very difficult. Although food volume may not be a problem, food quality is. In fact, high-quality native food sources may not exist. With high-quality food sources so limited, herd density would need to be reduced far below what would be acceptable by hunters in order to reach the levels of herd health required of TDM.

A successful TDM program with acceptable hunter satisfaction parameters will most likely require supplemental feeding. Without supplemental feeding, criteria for what constitutes a trophy must be adjusted downward. No matter how low the herd density, when natural high-quality food sources are limited, it's difficult for deer to reach their full potential body size and antler development.

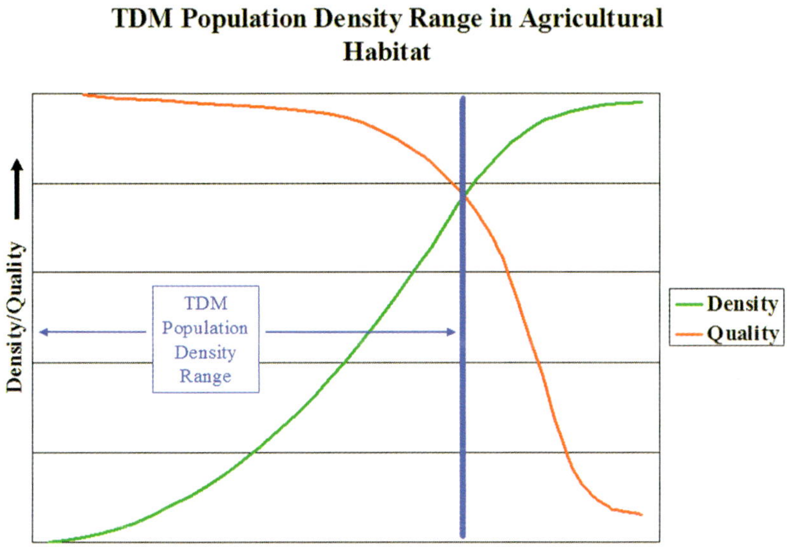

Figure 9. Agricultural habitat is where TDM is most successful. That is why the Midwest's agricultural regions produce so many record-book bucks. Nearly unlimited volumes of high-quality foods are available and these habitats allow a sizeable density that remains within the desired density/quality range. Because a truly record-class buck is rare, even in high-quality habitat, the ability to support higher deer densities increases the probability of one's occurrence on a property. More selective culling can be done to "weed out" undesirable traits while still leaving enough bucks to mature.

Agricultural habitat is where TDM is most successful. That is why the agricultural regions of the Midwest produce so many record-book bucks.

few negative social interactions (because of the low-density herd), reproductive and fawn survival rates are very high. Because does are in excellent physical condition, milk production and subsequent fawn body growth should be maximized.

Trophy management is not about overall herd health and social dynamics, or even hunter satisfaction. It is about producing the largest-antlered bucks possible. Intense population control is required to ensure a yield of fully mature top-end bucks each year. Genetic manipulation through culling is also used in TDM programs.

Managing a TDM herd requires in-depth knowledge and experience with local deer herds. Proper population numbers are derived by working backward by first determining the number of harvestable bucks desired, and then figuring how many fawns must be produced to achieve that goal. Several other factors must be added into the calculations to decide the appropriate beginning number.

Here are some examples. To produce a constant number of fully mature, top-end bucks, you must first determine how many male fawns to produce each year. Approximately 50 percent of fawns will be male, so the number of fawns needed to encourage a buck-rich environment is doubled immediately. Annual mortality also must be factored because a percentage of bucks in each age-class will die from causes other than hunting each year. In addition, at approximately three to four years of age, bucks are old enough to express some of their genetic potential, but not be old enough to be dominant breeders. (Older, bigger bucks in the herd will be the dominant breeders.) Because top-end bucks are the goal, 3- to 4-year-old bucks that appear to have less-than-desirable antler development may be culled from the herd. These culled bucks also must be accounted for, which is why the equation is worked somewhat backward. Additionally, to complicate matters, this entire calculated population must remain below the inflection point on the Herd Density to Herd to Habitat Quality graph.

In a TDM herd where total deer density must be kept below the inflection point, only enough does are kept in the population to produce the required number of fawns each year. Having more does than are needed for reproduction purposes simply takes valuable food resources away from the buck population, which might hamper antler development and thus be detrimental to the overall success of the TDM program.

In addition to concerns over herd density, doe populations in a TDM program are kept very young. Does older than age 2½ are harvested. Similar to the hybridization of plants, to increase the rate at which "desirable" genetic traits are concentrated within the population, the offspring of parents expressing desired genetic traits are used in the next generation of selective breeding. These offspring have the greatest possibility of displaying more of the desired traits and are more likely to pass those traits onto the next generation. If "better" bucks are being produced and allowed to breed, then their doe offspring should be allowed to breed while older does are removed. These older does were a product of breeding when less-desirable genetic selection was achieved within the herd.

In a TDM program only enough does are kept in the herd to meet buck-fawn production requirements. Adult sex ratios heavily favor bucks-often as much as three-to-one-which causes the rut to be very short. The shorter rut reduces stress on breeding bucks. In addition, mature bucks subordinate most of the younger bucks. These subordinated bucks have little chance of participating in the rut, reducing rut stress among this group. Instead of burning essential body reserves chasing does all fall and winter, less-than-mature buck body weights are maintained going into the winter stress period. These bucks start the next growing season with a "full tank," so to speak. In these cases, nutrition is used to further bone and antler growth, as opposed to filling depleted reserves and playing "catch up."

A TDM program allows a higher percentage of bucks to reach full maturity compared to MBHM or QDM. With the abundant food resources available to low-density herds, these fully mature bucks have an excellent chance of expressing their full potential. With each buck reaching their potential, bucks with the "best" genetics should be the dominant breeder bucks; hence natural selection can work most efficiently, that is the "best" genetics are passed on at the highest rate.

The TDM program has only a few biological downsides. First, with a high percentage of fully mature bucks, dominance competition is exaggerated. This intense competition can increase physical and social stresses in the buck population, and may result in higher-than-normal buck mortality caused by violent dominance battles. This is especially true when a herd progresses toward a mature age structure. For example, if a TDM program is initiated and progresses to a point where several 3-year-old bucks are present, there will be intense activity to establish dominance. However, once the herd matures to where all age classes are represented, even the 3- and 4-year-olds will

Photo by George Barnett

Because of the density of older bucks in a TDM herd, mortality rates from fighting typically exceed those found in MBHM or QDM herds.

be subordinated to some extent. Many deer breeders that maintain 10-plus 3-year-old bucks in a pen place one 5-year-old or older buck in the pen. Just the presence of the 5-year-old buck significantly reduces fighting among the 3-year-olds. The same relationships are found in wild, free-ranging herds.

Similar to how the low buck age structure of an MBHM herd disrupts natural social interactions, the artificially low doe age structure of a TDM herd may also interfere with normal social interactions. A very young doe population may not be physically mature enough for the natural processes of dominance and subordination to become established. The does may simply be too young to establish a "pecking order" within their social units, and a pecking order is just as important within the doe population as it is within the buck population.

The TDM Hunting Experience

Certainly, TDM herds offer the highest chance of seeing and harvesting record-book caliber bucks. Although very short, the rut in a TDM herd is intense, and much of the rutting activity occurs during daylight (legal hunting hours). Also, the ultra-intense competition for breeding rights influences bucks to make large amounts of rut sign. Huge signpost rubs and communal scrapes are common, and patterning mature bucks is easier as they produce a large amount of rut sign.

Hunting techniques such as rattling, decoying, and calling work exceptionally well in TDM herds. This is regularly displayed in hunting shows filmed on trophy managed properties. The extreme competition between older bucks vying for access to the few does causes quick and often violent reactions to these calling techniques.

Photo by George Barnett

Hunters in a Trophy Deer Management program must be well versed in aging deer on the hoof.

On the negative side, TDM herds offer very low deer densities, so hunters may see far fewer deer than they are accustomed. However, extensive supplemental feeding can keep deer densities and deer-observation rates higher.

Harvest guidelines are strict within a TDM program. Hunters must be able to identify harvestable, fully mature bucks from high-quality middle-aged bucks, and even more importantly, be able to control their trigger finger. Most hunters have never been in the position of passing up bucks that would be considered trophies elsewhere.

Is TDM Right for You?

Most hunters dream of hunting a trophy-managed herd, as depicted on TV and in hunting magazines. However,

Photo by George Barnett

Because of the land, resources, and knowledge necessary to conduct a successful Trophy Deer Management program, it is well beyond the reach of most hunters.

achieving this type of herd is more difficult than most hunters imagine. Large tracts of land, high-fences, the assistance of professionals, possibly intense year-round supplemental feeding, and hired hands to control equipment and culling projects are time-consuming and costly. For most hunters, this type of experience is beyond their pocketbooks.

TDM Implementation and Maintenance

TDM can be difficult to implement. Lowering a herd to below the inflection point is easier said than done. Adult does, when exposed to intense hunting pressure, become difficult to harvest. Arguably, an adult doe living under intense hunting pressure may be the toughest animal in North America to harvest. The increases in fawn production and survival mean a high annual doe harvest. Without the high harvest, the increased reproductive success would keep driving the population toward and above the inflection point.

TDM requires extreme control over the deer herd, which often means a high-fence, not necessarily to keep big bucks in, but to keep the neighbors' deer out. The genetic culling of bucks and the tight control of the doe population can be fruitless if outside deer constantly filter into the managed property.

A great deal of knowledge is required, either personally or from consulting professionals, to run the program and judge the quality and age of bucks. Bucks that are not expressing the desired antler growth should be culled because they are eating resources that could go toward the growth and development of other deer. Many mistakes occur when inexperienced hunter/managers practice selective culling. What may look like an 8-point cull buck to some may be a well-developed young

Photo by George Barnett

A Trophy Deer Management program requires extreme control of the deer herd, and that usually requires a high fence.

buck in body size, yet still needing a few years of growth before reaching his maximum antler potential. Getting bucks into the older age-class is hard when excited trigger fingers are the primary management tool.

One of the major limiting factors to implementing a TDM program is cost. Land base, possible high-fencing, population censusing, establishing and maintaining adequate food resources, and professional wildlife-management advice can generate a sizeable annual price tag. True TDM is often far outside the budgets of most hunters. In addition, it can't be stated enough that attention to detail is one of many essential keys in successful TDM programs. Although a TDM program may be possible on your property, you must first ensure your goals match your resources before embarking on the venture. Counsel and guidance from experienced biologists and managers can help cut time and costs as opposed to learning it "the hard way."

Photo by George Barnett

Chapter 10

Record Keeping

Previously we described the difference between the various forms of management and the herd conditions they produce. We also listed tips for how to implement each of these management practices. What we haven't discussed in detail is the process of tracking management progress.

Hunters can use several methods to track progress, although some are better than others. The number of bucks harvested may be great data for evaluating hunter satisfaction, but it doesn't tell much about what is going on with the deer herd. Each form of management is geared toward producing a specific herd structure and density, and hunters/managers must track their herd's progress toward those goals. Collecting data is the only way to accomplish this objective.

Observation Data

For tracking herd performance, observation and harvest are the two basic types of data collection. Observation data is information collected by hunters while they hunt, and is basically a tally of deer seen during the hunting season. These data can help track changes in herd composition, such as annual fawn production and adult sex ratios.

At a minimum, the following information should be recorded every time someone hunts the property:

- Date
- Number of antlered bucks observed
- Number of adult does observed
- Number of fawns (including button bucks) observed
- Number of deer that could not be identified as an antlered buck, adult doe, or fawn. That includes any antlerless deer that could not be identified as an adult doe or a fawn. (We call these "unidentified deer" or "unids".)

By tallying the number of antlered bucks seen during a season and comparing that to the number of adult does seen, hunters/managers can produce an "observed adult sex ratio." For example, if hunters saw 10 antlered bucks and 30 adult does during the hunting season, that is an observed adult sex ratio of one antlered buck to every three adult does, or more commonly expressed as "a 1:3 buck-to-doe ratio."

The observed fawn recruitment rate numbers are produced by comparing the number of fawns observed to the number of adult does. The observed fawn recruitment rate is expressed as a percentage. For example, if hunters observed 15 fawns and 30 adult does, the observed fawn recruitment is 50 percent. The number of fawns are divided by the number of adult does, and the product is multiplied by 100 [(fawns/does)x100]. To help visualize this number, imagine the fawn recruitment rate is based on the number of fawns observed

Photo by George Barnett

When bucks are heavily pressured, hunters often must find limited access areas to observe mature bucks.

per 10 adult does. If one fawn is observed per 10 adult does, recruitment is 10 percent. If five fawns are observed per those 10 adult does, the fawn recruitment rate is 50 percent. If eight fawns are observed per 10 adult does, the recruitment rate is 80 percent.

With observation data, questions arise about the accuracy of data derived from daylight sightings. Do observed ratios really exist in the herd? In some situations, the answer is probably no. Many factors influence daylight observations of deer, such as hunting/harvest pressure. If hunters place heavy pressure on bucks for years while applying little harvest pressure on does, observation data may be skewed. Under light harvest pressure does may be very active during daylight. For example, a hunter from a club we started working with reported that during a full weekend hunters saw approximately 200 antlerless deer in food plots but no antlered bucks. Does this mean the club's land has an adult sex ratio of 200 does per 0 bucks? No. First, many of those antlerless deer were fawns, and fawns are not used in adult sex-ratio calculations. Remember, it is the adult sex ratio, which means only deer 1½ years old or older are included in the calculations. In addition, this club had a history of heavy buck harvests while protecting does. Any antlered buck stepping into a food plot was harvested immediately. Bucks learned to avoid behavior that would get them killed. Does and fawns, however, learned they had nothing to fear from feeding in those plots during daylight. Hence, they were active and observable during legal hunting hours, and they were over represented in observation data.

Skewed observation data are common when harvest pressure is placed on one sex. However, these errors tend to disappear when hunters place harvest pressure on both sexes. In addition, exact fawn-recruitment and sex-ratio numbers are not as important as their trends over time. These trends help you track progress. Are conditions getting better? Are you getting closer to your goals? If the methods used to collect these data are consistent, trends will be accurate and can be used for management decisions.

One common error in observation data is the misidentification of fawns as adult does. Many hunters generically classify any deer without antlers as a "doe." However, in a healthy herd, half of the antlerless deer seen may be fawns. Therefore, it is important to assign any antlerless deer that cannot be positively identified as an "unidentified deer" instead of arbitrarily calling it a "doe." Distinguishing fawns from adult does is an educational process, and hunters get better with experience.

Another common question about observation data is "How do I make sure I'm not counting the same deer twice?" A season's worth of observation data is not a census of your deer herd. These numbers simply provide relative information on the ratio of observed deer. Once harvest pressure is equally applied to both sexes, each deer will be seen about the same number of times on average, producing accurate ratios.

Additional Observation Data

The observation data listed earlier are the minimum data to collect. However, other pieces of information are useful, such as the time all hunters start and stop hunting each time they go afield. These time data aid in analyzing differences in morning, midday and evening deer activity, as well as deer-observation rates. Deer observation rates are calculated (deer seen per hunting hour) by dividing the number of deer seen by the number of hours hunted. For example, if hunters spend 100 hours hunting a given property in a single year and they saw 20 deer, that would be a deer observation rate of 0.2 deer seen per hunting hour (20 deer/100 hours = 0.2 deer per hour).

Observation rates are important because they tell you how often deer are seen. They also eliminate differences in the number of deer seen because of hunting more or less time each year. Hunters often have years in which they see twice as many deer as they did the previous year. Just looking at the number of observed bucks can suggest there were twice as many bucks on the property. However, what hunters don't realize is they may have been hunting twice as much as in the previous year. By analyzing the number of deer observed compared to the number of hours hunted, they see they actually had the same buck observation rate both years.

Another piece of observation data to collect is the number of antler points on each buck. Although antler points are not always good age indicators, young bucks generally have fewer points than older bucks. By tracking the average number of points per buck, you can obtain some idea of the buck age structure. The higher the average number of antler points per buck, the older and/or healthier the buck population.

You also might include data that identify which deer meet harvest guidelines. This allows you to track the observation rate of harvestable deer. Even weather and moon conditions can be added to observation data. Many hunters want to know if specific weather or moon conditions produce more daylight deer activity. Collecting these data can provide detailed

Recording and analyzing observed antler point data provides an indicator of the herd's buck age structure.

Adding lunar and climatic conditions to your observation cards can provide you with custom deer movement data for your area.

information on how deer react to specific climatic or lunar conditions.

Harvest Data

You must also collect harvest data to track the progress of any management program, because it provides detailed deer-condition information that is critical to assessing herd health. The minimum data to collect from each harvested deer includes:

- Date of harvest
- Sex
- Age
- Live and field-dressed weight (if both cannot be acquired, pick one and be consistent)
- Buck antler dimensions (points, beam length, spread, and antler score)
- Doe lactation status

From these data hunters can calculate critical indicators of herd health. Obviously average body weights must be calculated by sex and age-class. Doe lactation status is simply whether the doe had milk in her udder. Although fawns are born in late spring or summer, a doe that produces and raises a fawn for several weeks continues to have milk in her udder for several months, even if her fawn did not survive the summer. Comparing lactation rates against observed fawn recruitment helps identify late-summer fawn mortality. Doe lactation rates also help identify nutritionally stressed herds, because many fawns born in such herds do not survive long after birth.

Photo by George Peacon

Collecting harvest data, especially the age of every deer harvested, is essential to a successful management program.

Photo by George Barnett

Chapter 11

A Case Study

The following case study is adapted from an article in the August 2003 issue of *Quality Whitetails*, the journal of the Quality Deer Management Association (QDMA). We think this case study is an excellent example of how herds respond to different harvest rates. It also shows how observation and harvest data are used to track a program's progress.

Case Study

We conducted this study on a 7,300-acre block of private property in west-central Georgia. The habitat of the study area was mixed-age pine and hardwoods timber, with few openings and an extensive closed canopy. Our only habitat changes were developing a few food plots, primarily to provide deer observation and harvest locations. This food-plot acreage accounted for less than 1 percent of the total acreage and was developed with minimal equipment. For those who don't have the proper equipment, mowing, disking, and planting can generally be contracted at $24 to $35 per hour in most rural areas. During the project, we also improved a small percentage of the forest through thinnings and controlled burns

Our purpose was to study the effects of different harvest intensities on the health and composition of two similar deer herds. To document differences produced by harvests strategies, it was vital to use two large sections of land, with similar

During this project, we improved a small percentage of the forest through thinnings and controlled burns.

Minimal habitat improvements can increase the nutritional plane for your deer herd.

habitat and deer density/health parameters. During the project, both sections were hunted by the same group of hunters using the same hunting techniques to eliminate bias produced by different techniques or levels of hunting skill.

We split the study area along a gravel road and designated the property to the east as "Unit A" and the area to the west as "Unit B."

Initially, we tried to implement a harvest density on one unit that was twice as high as the other, with the harvest on both primarily comprised of females. Unit A was chosen as the "high" deer harvest unit, and we attempted an annual harvest rate of 12.8 does/mile^2 (1 doe/50 acres). Unit B was scheduled to receive half of that harvest density, or 6.4 does/mile^2 (1 doe/100 acres).

When heavy hunting pressure is put on does, hunter success eventually decreases as does become more wary.

However, harvesting large numbers of does for several consecutive years is easier to conceive than accomplish. Under intense harvest pressure, does become wary of common hunting techniques and hunter success decreases. Therefore, during the project's four-year run, the annual harvest density on Unit A only averaged 10.1 does/mile^2 (1 doe/63.2 acres), and Unit B averaged 6.0 does/mile^2 (1 doe/107.1 acres). In both units, most deer harvested were females: 82.1 percent in Unit A and 89.0 percent in Unit B.

When comparing herd-composition data, the most obvious difference between the two units was the adult sex ratio. Observation data indicated the adult sex ratio increased more quickly in the higher harvest density Unit A (Figure 11-1). Unit A's annual observed adult sex ratio increased from 0.9 bucks per doe to 1.8 bucks per doe. In fact, the number of observed bucks per doe in Unit A averaged 140 percent higher than in Unit B annually. Nevertheless, the fact that observed bucks outnumbered does in Unit B in the project's final year suggests the lower deer harvest rate implemented in Unit B eventually produced the desired result, although the lower harvest density may have simply delayed and muted the response.

Observed fawn recruitment (the ratio of observed fawns to adult does, expressed as a percentage) also differed between the two areas. Although recruitment at both areas improved during the project, Unit A consistently produced higher observed fawn recruitment numbers than Unit B each year (Figure 11-2). The lactation rates of harvested 2½-year-old and older does also increased dramatically during the experiment. However, unlike fawn recruitment, we detected no substantial differences in adult doe lactation rates between the two areas.

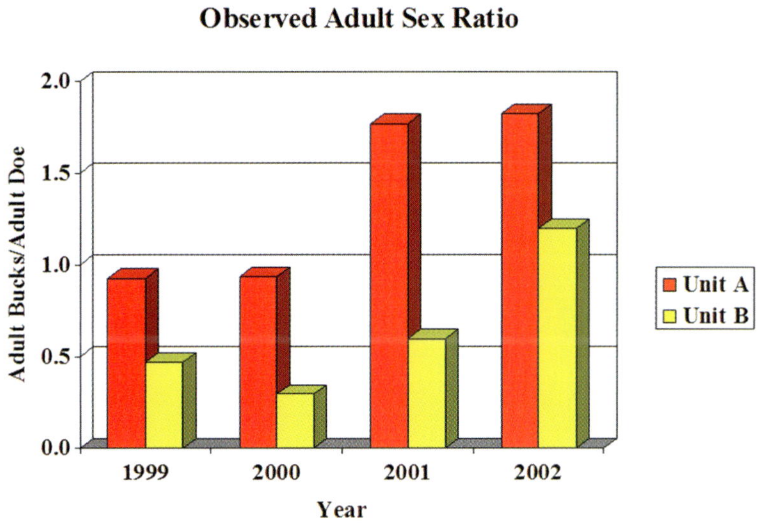

Figure 11-1. Observed Adult Sex Ratio, 1999-2002.

The observed adult sex ratio in Unit A, the higher harvest density, was consistently better than in Unit B, averaging 140 percent more observed adult bucks than adult does throughout the period. The lower harvest in Unit B eventually improved the observed adult sex ratio, but these improvements took longer and were less pronounced than in Unit A.

This suggests that although the health and, ultimately, the reproductive success of both areas increased dramatically, fawn survival was greater under the higher density harvest strategy in Unit A.

Harvested doe body weights are another indicator used to track herd health. During the last two years of our experiment, doe body weights per age-class averaged 3 to 9 percent greater in Unit A than in Unit B. Interestingly, these higher body weights were limited to does born during the experiment

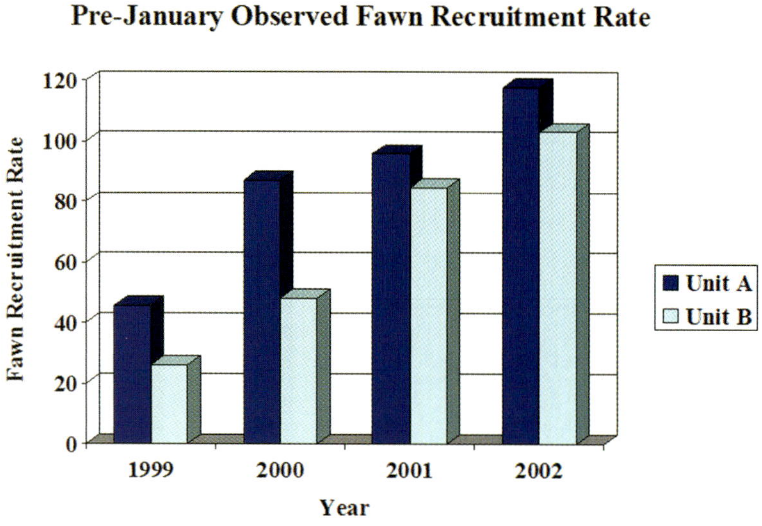

Figure 11-2. Pre-January Observed Fawn Recruitment, 1999-2002.

The observed fawn recruitment rate ([observed fawns / observed adult does] x 100) improved dramatically in both units. However, the higher harvest of females from Unit A produced consistently higher fawn recruitment values throughout the project.

Data used in this graph were limited to observations during September through December. These limitations were used for two reasons. First, the heavy harvest of adult does during late December through the winter months left many orphaned fawns, which are often active during daylight. Their repeated observations would have skewed the data. Second, fawns can be difficult to identify after December because they can put on enough body weight to look as large as an adult doe.

(4½-year-old or younger does). Does born before the experiment began (does 5½ years old or older) did not display differences in body weights (Figure 11-3). This also supports the theory that the stresses a deer experiences early in life may affect its health throughout its lifetime. This may have major implications not only for body growth, but for lifetime reproductive success in does and antler production in bucks.

Whenever doe harvest rates are debated, hunters often worry that too many does will be harvested. One way to test for doe overharvest is to examine the age structure of the harvested does, especially those harvested after several years of a high harvest. (This analysis is accurate unless immature does are selected for harvest. However, most hunters select the larger-bodied, more-mature does.) During the fourth year of the experiment, the harvested doe age structure indicated that 35 percent of does harvested in Unit A and 40 percent of does harvested in Unit B were fully mature (5½ years old or older). When 35 to 40 percent of a population is in the fully mature age classes, that is a very old age structure and does not indicate overharvest.

Of course, every harvest/management strategy produces positive and negative results, and high doe harvest strategies are no exception. What were the negatives of the higher doe harvest rates?

As mentioned, once intense harvest pressure is placed on a herd, deer become extremely wary of human/hunter contact. They learn to avoid common hunting situations, such as entering food plots and other open areas during daylight. This increased wariness affects deer observations and harvests. In this experiment, both areas experienced decreased deer

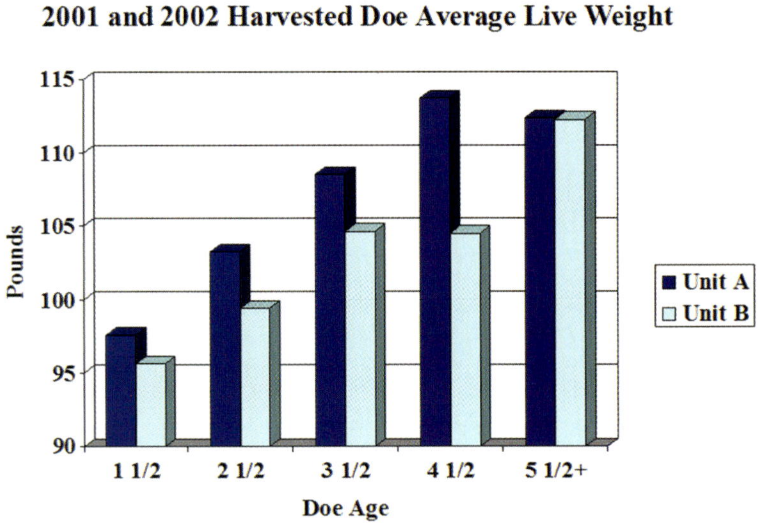

Figure 11-3. Harvested Doe Average Live Weights, 2001-2002.

The average live weights of adult does in Unit A during the final two years of the project (with the exception of does 5½ years old or older) were higher than the same-aged does in Unit B. The higher deer harvests of Unit A likely pushed the deer density of Unit A farther left on the Density to Quality Relationship graph, increasing herd quality and health.

The oldest does (5½-year-olds and older) did not show a difference in body weight between the two areas. These does were born before the project began, and the nutritionally stressed conditions they were born into may have stunted their growth. Nutrition and food resources in the first year of life are critical to growth potential as an adult.

observation and harvest rates over time, and predictably, the higher harvest pressure in Unit A produced the greatest declines. During the project's last four years, observation rates declined 45 percent in Unit A and 20 percent in Unit B, while harvest rates declined 44 percent and 40 percent in Units A and B, respectively.

Most decreases in observation/harvest rates were linked to the doe population. Buck observation rates were substantially higher in Unit A than Unit B. During the last years of this project, buck observation rates averaged 90 percent higher in Unit A than Unit B (Figure 11-4). Not until the last year did buck observation rates in Unit B catch up to those in Unit A. The high harvest pressure on does did not appear to hurt buck observations.

Interestingly the observation rates of bucks with 10 or more antler points was much higher in Unit A than Unit B, with the observation rates trending generally upward over time in Unit A and downward in Unit B (Figure 11-5). During the project's third year (2001), bucks with 10 or more antler points were observed in Unit A with 180 percent more frequency than in Unit B.

Several reasons explain this difference in large-antlered buck-observation rates between the two areas. First, there may have been more 10-plus-point bucks in Unit A. The higher harvest density may have decreased the deer density to the point that increased health allowed bucks to express more of their genetic antler potential. Secondly, the lower adult sex ratio of Unit B during the project may have reduced breeding competition enough that the oldest/largest bucks were not as

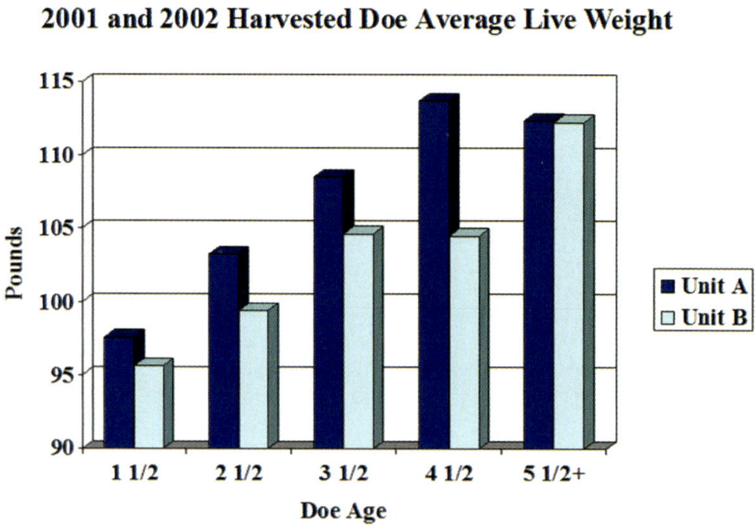

Figure 11-4. Annual Buck Harvest Rates, 1999 - 2002.

During the last years of this project, buck observation rates averaged 90 percent higher in Unit A (higher harvest) than in Unit B. The higher doe harvest of Unit A drastically improved the adult sex ratio, producing competition among bucks for breeding rights. This increased competition drives bucks toward more daylight movement, making them more observable.

active during daylight, reducing the rate at which they were observed by hunters.

Obviously, a lot more information can be shared from this project. However, there has been talk in certain regions recently that doe harvests may not be necessary or a sound management tool. We had a project in South Carolina for 11 years where we also followed high doe harvest guidelines. Eleven

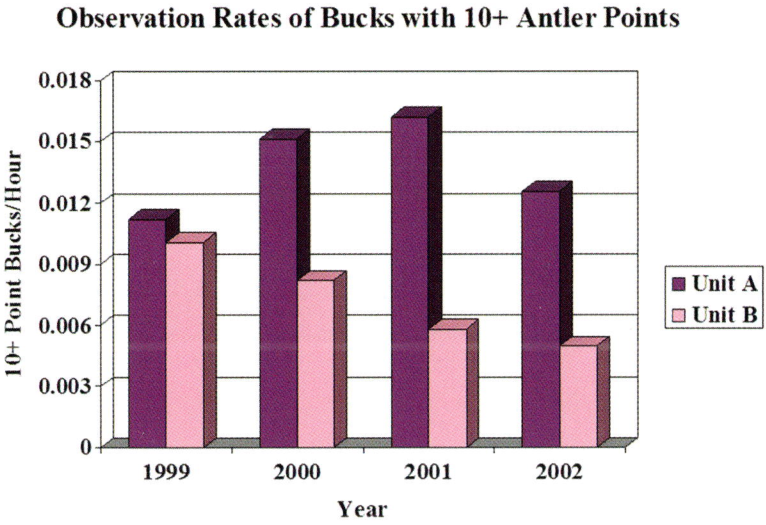

Figure 11-5. Annual observation rates of bucks with 10 or more antler points, 1999 - 2002.

Hunters in Unit A consistently observed 10-plus-point bucks more frequently than hunters in Unit B. In 2001, the observation rate of 10-plus-point bucks was 180 percent higher in Unit A than in Unit B. Throughout the project 10-plus-point buck observation rates in Unit A generally trended upward year to year, while observation rates declined year to year in Unit B.

years of intensive data on a hunted free-ranging deer herd is rare. Both projects yielded similar results:

- Harvest management (trigger-finger management) is an effective tool for improving age structures and adult sex ratios. The more aggressive the doe harvest and the passing of bucks, the more rapidly herd demographics can change.

- Minimal percentages ($\frac{1}{2}$ percent of total acreage) of food plots can make a significant difference in herd health. We establish our food plots by selecting quality forage crops, and liming and fertilizing per soil-test recommendations. We control weeds with herbicides and/or mowing. Our rule of thumb is to develop the maximum acreage in food plots we can afford to establish and maintain properly. This is better than developing twice the acreage in plots that are not properly maintained.

- Intensive habitat management, genetic manipulation, etc., are all management tools that can be used to improve deer herd quality. However, quality deer herds and high-quality hunting can be established and maintained by trigger-finger (herd density, sex ratio, and age structure) and food-plot management. This type of deer management is the cornerstone of Quality Deer Management and is available to most hunters across America. Depending on the size of your hunting lands, you can meet your goals sooner by forming cooperatives with your hunting neighbors.

As deer hunters, we are also deer managers. When we are in the field, we make the ultimate management decisions. If a quality deer herd and a quality hunting experience are your

Collecting data is an essential part of any deer management program.

goals, then intelligent harvest decisions with a little sweat and hard work are the keys that open the door to more enjoyable times afield.

Photo by George Barnett

Chapter 12

Summary

Interest in specialized management has changed the face of deer hunting. Hunters now realize suitcase hunts-traveling long distances-are no longer required to experience quality hunting. Under a well-designed and implemented management program, local hunting lands may provide the experiences hunters desire. Depending on habitat limitations, MBHM, QDM, or TDM experiences can be created near home-wherever home may be.

Our client, and good friend, the late Bill Cheatum hunted on a lease in South Florida. He was dedicated to sound deer management even though his neighbors and most of his peers often said, "This area won't produce quality deer." Bill took a leadership role in convincing South Florida hunters that even low-productivity habitat can produce quality bucks and healthy herds.

Stories like that explain why we wrote this book. We wanted to provide an educational tool that helps hunters make sound management decisions on their lands, and just as importantly, helps protect our passion: deer hunting. Hunting is a privilege, not a God-given right. To protect the privilege to hunt, we believe hunters must be good stewards of the wildlife resources. As much as we hunters and managers may not like to admit it, our legal ability to hunt is held in the hands of the voting public, most of whom do not hunt. If hunting serves a valuable role to the nonhunting public, it likely will remain

This great South Florida buck was harvested by the late Bill Cheatum, and was the result of a dedicated deer and habitat management program on his lease.

legal. If hunters are not perceived as managers and do not provide a service to nonhunters, hunting's future is questionable. Hunting will only survive if it is wisely used as a tool for managing wildlife resources.

Wise management of the white-tailed deer resource includes maintaining herds below the density that would inflict severe habitat damage. The deer, the habitat, and all the other animals that use the habitat deserve no less. We also believe wise management includes holding deer densities below the level causing human-deer conflicts-the social carrying capacity. Farmers and local residents deserve no less. We believe that when hunters have a basic understanding of deer-herd dynamics and factors influencing herd health and performance, they make better decisions at the moment of truth. And by making intelligent decisions, they become not just consumers, but conscientious managers of that resource.

Wildlife agencies play a vital role in deer management. Many agencies are adjusting seasons and bag limits to produce healthy herds. But agencies can only do so much. Hunters must realize *they* are the actual deer managers. Within state regulations, *they* are the ones deciding which animals are removed and which animals stay in the herd. Only those pulling the trigger have that power.

Just like deer herds and habitat, hunting is ever-changing. As we mentioned, hunters must learn to become managers-not just mere consumers. If readers remember just one concept from this book, it should be the constant realization that every time they pull the trigger or pass up a harvest opportunity, they have made a management decision that affects the health and productivity of the local herd for years.

So how do deer hunters decide which management program is best for their hunting lands? When developing a management plan, whether it is MBHM, QDM or TDM, make sure your objectives realistically match your budget. The habitat (current and after improvements), time availability, and the entire group's willingness to participate are also essential factors. The more intense your management program, the more resources and commitment will be required. Satisfaction with any endeavor is a function of expectations. Make sure your expectations are realistic. Don't expect to grow 300-pound deer in southern Florida. Likewise, don't try to hold 60 deer per square mile in Northern forests. Do not expect to grow

Photo by George Barnett

Wise management of the white-tailed deer resource includes maintaining herds below the density that would inflict severe habitat damage. The deer, the habitat, and all of the other animals deserve no less.

record-book deer on 100 acres when your neighbors follow harvest guidelines that proclaim, "When it's brown, it's down." Outside of agricultural areas, don't expect to keep a high deer density while producing large bucks. The density-quality relationship will stifle your efforts.

Although we have discussed the density-to-quality relationship throughout this book, the issue is so critical we ask your indulgence in discussing this relationship one more time. The following example may help you choose which type of management is possible on a given property. Graph 12-1 displays the population density range appropriate for each of the three primary habitat types. Notice that each bar represents the maximum herd size for the local habitat conditions. This maximum size does not represent the "carrying capacity." It represents the maximum herd size that could occur before the herd stops growing because of food shortages and other limitations, such as negative deer-deer social interactions. In addition, we caution you to remember that this maximum herd size depends heavily on habitat quality. For instance, a Standard Model habitat composed of 10 percent agriculture will have a different maximum herd size than one composed of 30 percent agriculture.

If you believe we advocate QDM as the best management option, you are not wrong. We believe QDM produces the healthiest and most natural herd structure. That doesn't mean other forms of management aren't biologically sound. MBHM and TDM are biologically sound when practiced correctly.

For those interested in creating the hunting experience offered by MBHM, just remember that practicing MBHM doesn't make you immune from having to harvest antlerless deer.

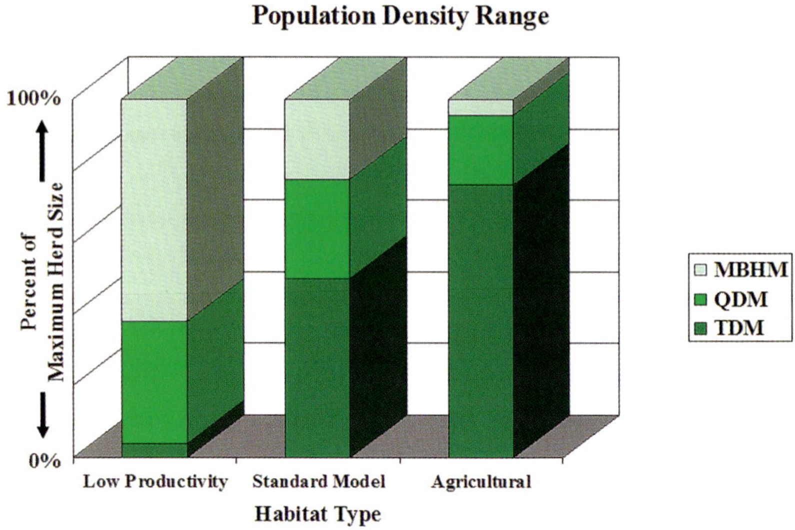

Figure 12-1. The density-to-quality relationship should not be overlooked when evaluating management options. Each habitat will have a range of deer population densities that is best suited to each form of management.

TDM opportunities in a Low Productivity habitat are extremely limited. The high-quality food resources required for effective TDM are rapidly depleted at even the lowest herd density. Even the practice of QDM requires Low Productivity habitat deer herds to be held at much lower densities than the habitat could support. A large range of herd densities in Low Productivity habitat are practical for MBHM, however.

Standard Model habitat provides more opportunities for all three forms of management. TDM herd densities can be achieved in a Standard Model habitat, although depending on food production, these lower herd densities may be well below the level hunters find acceptable. QDM shines as a management option for Standard Model habitat, with the potential for high-quality herds and acceptable deer sightings for hunters.

Cont. from page 214. Agricultural habitat provides a wide latitude of herd densities that fall within the TDM range, and it is in Agricultural habitat that TDM will be most successful.

The herd still needs to be controlled in an MBHM program. In fact, herd density control is probably more critical under MBHM than the other two options, considering the herd will constantly be held near the point at which habitat damage could occur. One or two years of inadequate doe harvests could produce long-term or even permanent habitat damage, severely limiting the area's ability to produce healthy deer in the future. Maintaining the herd below the habitat damage level is critical in an MBHM program, although the number of females that need to be harvested annually will be lower than in a QDM or TDM program.

For those interested in practicing QDM, remember that quality management is far more involved than simply passing up opportunities to harvest young bucks. Little progress can be made without harvesting does to balance the adult sex ratio. Most areas will also require habitat management to maximize herd potential.

Hunters interested in TDM must evaluate several considerations. How deep are your pockets? How much acreage do you have to work with and how much control do you have over the herd? Do you have access to the necessary trophy management expertise? Are few deer sightings and buck harvests acceptable?

Lastly, understanding hunting's role as a wildlife-management tool is critical for hunters and nonhunters alike. But

Photo by George Barnett

Hunters involved in deer management programs find it increases the hunt's recreational value. The hunt truly expands from a few days to year round involvement.

that doesn't mean deer management is all cold biology. Deer hunting and management should be fun. Every person defines fun differently. Some enjoy intensive data collection and campfire talk about adult sex ratios and fawn-recruitment numbers. Others only wish to collect minimal amounts of data to make management decisions. Deer management should be an integral part of an enjoyable hunting experience. It has been our experience that many hunters like being involved in deer management programs, and that it increases the hunt's recreational value. The hunt truly expands from a few days of hunting to year-round involvement. Hunters responding to opinion surveys clearly state their satisfaction with the overall hunting experience increases significantly by becoming an active deer manager; that is, being involved in habitat improvement, passing young bucks, collecting data, harvesting does, etc. We are constantly amazed by the number of hunters who-once involved in a management program-find the management itself is just as enjoyable as the hunting experiences it produces.

Chapter 13

My Easiest Hunt

I was raised among hunters. My mother always gave my father, my brother-in-law, and me our hunting licenses for Christmas. Before I was old enough to need a hunting license, one of my favorite toys was a double barrel, side by side, spring-action dart gun and a wind-up rabbit. I spent many hours shooting at that rabbit. As my skills progressed, I would place the rabbit where it would "run" between chairs and other furniture to limit my shot opportunities.

When I was in third grade, my Uncle Joe loaned me a single shot .410. My father, grandfather, and Uncle Joe were present when, after many, many misses, I harvested my first rabbit with that gun!

My father, grandfather, brother-in-law, and Uncle Joe taught me how to hunt. The days we spent hunting rabbits, quail, dove, and groundhogs were the foundation for my career. My lessons in wildlife ecology began before 'ecology' was a popular word. I began by learning from my mentors where rabbits and quail could be found based on the type of plants present. Their observations about game behavior and use of habitat have certainly proven invaluable.

These men and others were always present in my life. They were my friends and hunting buddies, but more importantly, they were my mentors. They lead by example. These men taught me to obey hunting seasons and limits. However, seasons and limits were not their guide. Doing what was right was their guide.

In my life, I've been blessed in many ways, including following my boyhood passion by becoming a wildlife biologist and working with white-tailed deer. This path took me to many colleges, jobs, locations, etc. Many times along the path of life I literally lost my way and strayed from my upbringing. However, the many hours that I spent with my mother, father, and other men who recognized Christ as their savior and "did what was right" helped me find my bearings in life. My life is now dedicated to serving Christ, loving my wife, and sharing Christ and my passion for His creation with our two daughters.

I encourage you to trust Christ as your savior. The process is so simple-admit that you are a sinner, believe in your heart that Jesus died for your sins, and commit your life to following Him. There is no hunt as important as finding Christ. Those of us who have found Christ should share Him. We should live our life in His light. We need to light the trail for others to bag the greatest trophy of life-eternal salvation!

My parents talked to me about Christ, and that was the most important lesson in my life. If you are a Christian, please be a mentor to others. Take a family member or friend hunting and speak to them about Christ. The only way to truly enjoy His creation is to know the Creator.

-Grant R. Woods
February, 2004

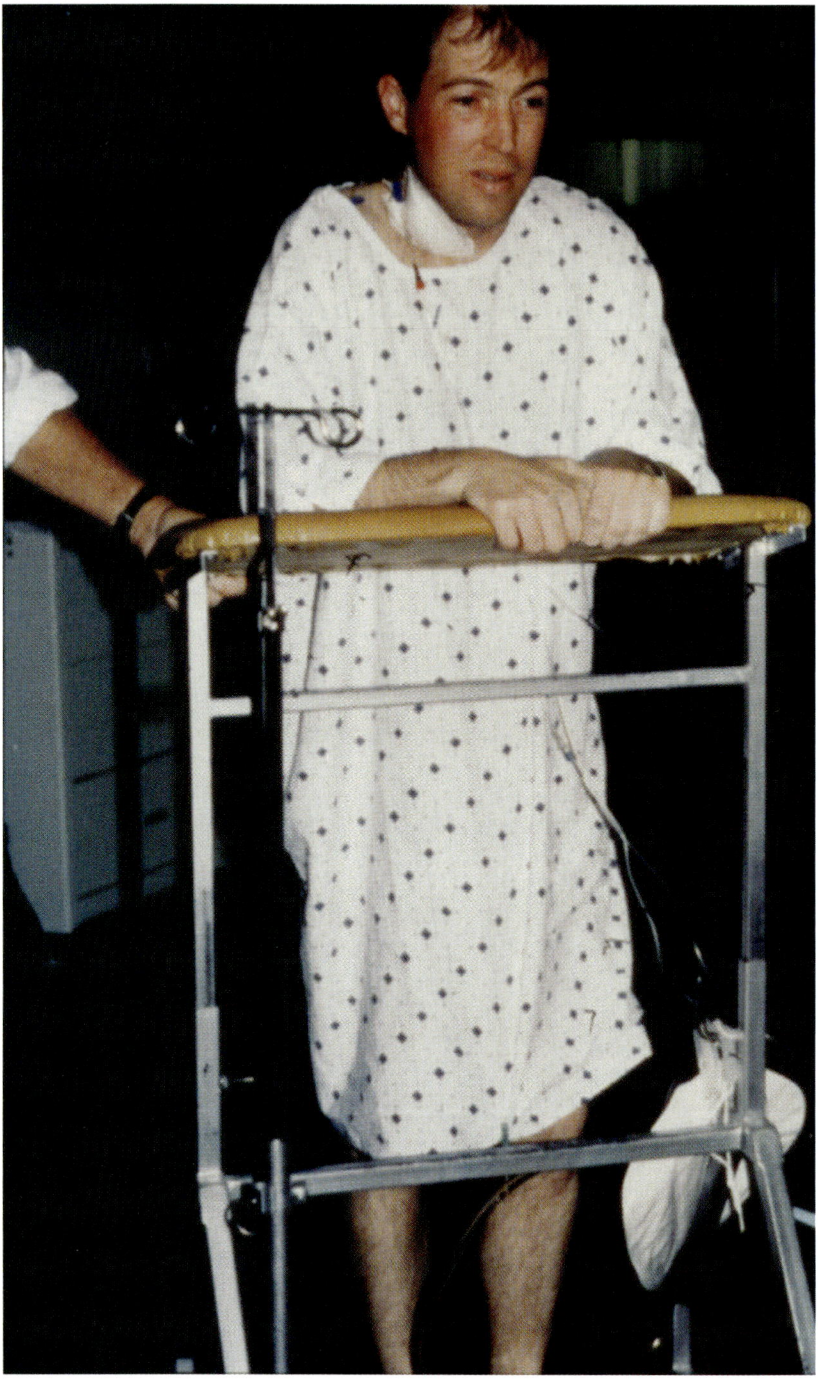

Chapter 14

Grant's Best Birthday Gift

My birthday is June 11th. However, I received my best birthday gift June 9, 1992. The path to receiving this gift began a decade earlier.

During summers while in college, I worked for the Bureau of Land Management in Elko, Nevada, as a wildlife technician. A requirement for this job was a physical, which included a urine sample. I went to a university student health center to undergo my physical. My urine sample showed above-normal amounts of protein. All I was concerned about was going west and working with mule deer! I convinced the doctor I would follow up three months later when I returned to school. He agreed and signed my physical. Let me state that I accept any blame for this lack of judgment.

I had a great summer. I learned much about mule deer habitat management. It was also a dry summer, with several hundred thousand acres of wild fires. This was before the national media sensationalized wild fires in Western states. Every able-bodied employee in the Elko Bureau of Land Management District was recruited to fight the fires. This included a crash course in firefighting techniques and a physical fitness test. I scored among the highest (most physically fit) in my district.

A few years later my sister Rebecca was diagnosed with kidney failure. She required kidney dialysis to remain alive.

My mother researched the option of kidney transplantation, and donated a kidney that saved my sister's life.

This crisis was my wake-up call. I remembered the protein in my urine and decided to have my kidney function checked. My total kidney function was only 23 percent. How could this be? By that time I had been on a wildfire team for portions of three summers. The rest of my summers had been spent high in the Rockies evaluating mule deer winter habitat and cutthroat trout stream conditions. I was in excellent shape!

The reality is that the human kidney functions above baseline requirements to maintain life. However, my doctors said kidney function usually decreases exponentially. Simply stated, once my kidneys began to fail, I would go downhill quickly. After two years of checkups with minimal decreases in kidney function, I thought the doctors were wrong. I decided my kidneys would not fail.

I remember the day I learned my doctor was correct. Within a six-month period my kidney function had decreased more than the previous two years. I was told I had only a few months before I would require dialysis to stay alive.

When I told my family, my sister Alice immediately volunteered to donate a kidney. She knew dialysis was a tough option. It is not only tough on the body, but it would drastically limit my chosen path in life. To be a practicing wildlife biologist-to work outside and with white-tailed deer throughout their range-I could not go on dialysis three times a week. Alice literally volunteered to give me the gift of life: a kidney.

My transplant was a success!! Alice and I had surgery on a Tuesday morning and we left the hospital the following Friday-only four days after our surgeries. Alice's gift of life is still allowing me to be a practicing wildlife biologist-almost 12 years later!!!

Years later, my mother-in-law was killed in a tragic accident. It was one of those accidents no one can explain. My wife was four months pregnant and we were building a house. It was a very rough time for Tracy (my wife), her family, and me. Tracy's mother suffered severe injuries to her brain, but the remainder of her body was unhurt and functioning. By law, her doctors were required to ask the family if they would consider allowing Tracy's mother to be an organ donor. Tracy's mother had told the family years before that if anything should happen to her that she wished to be an organ donor. The family knew her desire was to help others live a better life when she was at the end of her own. My wife's knowledge that her mother helped many people-people just like me who needed an organ to maintain life-was a great comfort during this crisis.

I'm asking you to learn the truth about organ donation. Please know that by only signing your driver's license you won't qualify as an organ donor. By law, organs can only be donated with the permission of the closest kin, or as stipulated in a trust (or some other legal document).

I'm asking you to decide to be an organ donor. Just as importantly, I'm asking you to talk to your family about your decision to be an organ donor. Your family may be the ones who have to make the donation decision. This year, a person will die every 17 minutes while waiting on an organ. These lives could be saved!!

When I leave this earth for the pearly gates, any of my organs that can be used are to be donated. Then, my body will go to the closest medical school to undergo research concerning the effects of transplant medications on the human body. Anything left is to be cremated, with the ashes placed in a salt lick. As many does as I have harvested, the least I can do is give something back to whitetails! Please, talk to your family now. Give the gift of life.

I began walking the morning after I received the gift of life-a kidney transplant. My sister (the donor) and I both left the hospital four days after the operation. Twelve years later, we are both enjoying great health.

-Grant Woods, Ph.D.
February, 2004

Notes

Notes

Notes

Notes

Notes

Notes

Notes

Notes

Notes